Simon Stock was born in Birmingham but moved to the Newcastle-upon-Tyne after entering medical school. He trained and worked as a surgeon in the NHS throughout the Northeast for 20 years before moving to the Isle of Man in 2001 and finally to Cambodia in 2012 where he continues to work as a volunteer surgeon. He is married with a daughter and three delightful grandchildren.

To all my patients, past, present and future.

Simon Stock

RANDOM MUSINGS OF A DISORDERLY MIND

AUSTIN MACAULEY PUBLISHERS®

LONDON * CAMBRIDGE * NEW YORK * SHARJAH

A CIP catalogue record for this title is available from the British Library.

ISBN 9781035884971 (Paperback)
ISBN 9781035884988 (ePub e-book)

www.austinmacauley.com

First Published 2024
Austin Macauley Publishers Ltd®
1 Canada Square
Canary Wharf
London
E14 5AA

My long-suffering wife and family for supporting me throughout my career, thus allowing the events portrayed herein to occur.

Dr. Gerlinda Lucas for persuading me to commit myself to print.

Introduction

I think that the greatest privilege of being a doctor is meeting patients. They can teach us so much, whether they are trying to or not. They let us into their lives in a way few others are allowed. Their trust challenges and humbles me. They can also be hilarious in more ways than you can imagine.

In this book, I hope to share some of the more extreme examples of my interactions with patients, both here in Cambodia, where I work as a volunteer surgeon, and from my former life in the Isle of Man and the UK. All the characters portrayed are real, and so, in some situations, I have altered names to protect those who may still be alive. In other cases, I have been deliberately vague about the circumstances under which we met.

I should issue a disclaimer—I believe all the information recorded here (apart from the exceptions above) is accurate, but some of it extends back over 40 years, so I accept that there may be one or two details that I have recalled incorrectly. Nevertheless, I do not believe that there is anything that is substantially different from the truth.

Of course, most of my daily work is what one might call routine, although I am not sure that the term routine is very applicable to medical practice, and the scenarios I present here are from many years of clinical practice. I suspect that there are many more that I have forgotten. There is no particular chronological order to the cases, but I have tried to group them together as themes.

The photographs used have all been taken with the permission of the patients involved, and I have done my best to ensure the anonymity of the persons depicted.

I should warn any squeamish readers that some of the descriptions and photographs in this book are rather graphic and leave little to the imagination, so you have been warned!

Chapter 1
Early Days

I had always wanted to be a doctor as long as I can remember, apart from a short period in which I thought it might be more fun to work in a shoe shop (the old-fashioned kind with all the shoeboxes stacked up on high shelves, and if there was one of those wonderful vacuum suction systems for transporting cylinders containing money and receipts to the remotely situated cashier's office, so much the better).

There was absolutely no one in my family who had been a doctor, although, for a time, my older brother went to medical school before deciding it wasn't for him. As a Christian, I also saw a career in medicine as a vocation rather than a job. I had always enjoyed science at school, having had some brilliant teachers, and so when the time came to apply to medical school, I got 2 conditional offers—one from Manchester and one from Newcastle on Tyne.

I visited both and felt much more welcome at Newcastle, where the medical school was smaller and more friendly than the one at Manchester (an intake of 130 students as opposed to 200 at Manchester). This proved to be a wise choice as the people of the North-East of England are a friendly bunch, and the atmosphere in the medical school under the Deanship of Professor John Walton reflected this.

The curriculum was also modern for its time (1970s), as there were attempts to introduce clinical exposure from an early stage as well as a short course, teaching nursing skills such as bed-making, dressing changes, personal care and so on. The first two years, however, were mainly theoretical and consisted of lectures and seminars with some practical work such as anatomical dissection and physiology experiments. We had many great lecturers, although some were a little eccentric.

One in particular only gave us a few lectures in clinical biochemistry. He had an extensive research background particularly focusing on chemical imbalances in cells in conditions like heart failure, the so-called sick cell syndrome. I remember one lecture (an hour long) when he was talking about this topic, and he was using a blackboard as his visual aid. He drew two lines on the board at right angles representing the axes of a graph, but no words, and he then drew a dot near the corner representing something I cannot remember.

Then, after a further 10 minutes or so of talking, he drew a second dot slightly above and to the right of the first one and that was it—the only thing he drew during the whole hour. Most of his lecture was also incomprehensible to us, who had not spent many years researching this particular topic!

We had an amusing insight into Geordie culture one day when our senior physiology lecturer, Professor Teddy Bear as we nicknamed him, walked in to start his lecture whilst one of the cleaning ladies was wiping the blackboard (this was a normal procedure between lectures). Unphased by the entrance of this eminent, white-coated professor, she said, "Sorry, pet, I won't be a minute!"

He seemed as unsurprised by receiving this familiar greeting as she was giving it. Most of our lectures were uncontroversial, some were humorous, but I can only recall one which caused some outrage, and this was from a gynaecologist who thought it would be entertaining to include some pornographic pictures in his presentation to supposedly illustrate his points. This led to several of the female students walking out in disgust, and he was reported to the course supervisor. I do not know the outcome of the complaint, but I do not recall seeing him for any more lectures thereafter.

Once we got to our third year, we spent mornings in the teaching hospitals on the wards, taking clinical histories and examining patients, but we would return to the lecture theatres in the afternoons for lectures on more clinical topics. Some of these were more interesting than others, and pathology was a subject I particularly enjoyed and have continued to do so ever since. This is an important topic as it is the study of the disease processes themselves and is a key to understanding a lot of what we see in clinical practice.

I recall two particular highlights of the course; one was the rather short course on forensic pathology by a home-office pathologist—think of a medical version of CSI complete with fascinating stories of murder investigations, unidentified dead bodies and so on, all backed up with graphic pictures! The other was nothing to do with the lectures, but rather about the lecturer.

One day, at the start of a new section of the pathology course, a very elegant young woman walked into the lecture hall to give the lecture. She was a cellular pathologist with an interest in aspects of bladder and prostate cancer. She also used to like to sit on the large bench across the front of the lecture theatre rather than stand behind it whilst delivering her lectures. I think at least half of the male students instantly developed a crush on her, and it was not at all uncommon to see a group come up to the front at the end of the lecture to ask questions, having suddenly developed a deep interest in pathology!

I sometimes wonder whether she was part of the inspiration for Mandy Kuypers in our yearbook (see below). It was certainly a notable departure from the more common middle-aged men who gave most of the lectures!

At the end of our third year, medical students had a three-month period over what would normally be the university's summer break, called an elective period. This allowed us to go somewhere else to work in virtually any aspect of medicine, and there were no restrictions on where we could go as long as we could organise and fund it ourselves. People chose different placements based on all sorts of criteria—some chose to go to exotic and far-flung locations like Transkei (now Eastern Cape) in South Africa, Central America or even Sunderland. Some people did laboratory medicine, whilst others did clinical work.

As a Christian, I wanted to work with medical missionaries in a rural setting and originally planned to go to Argentina with the South American Missionary Society. However, this was 1978, and tensions over the Falkland Islands were already beginning to build up and this, plus other factors resulted in my plans falling through. Eventually, I located a mission in the north of Paraguay, where a Scottish couple were working with the Edinburgh Medical Missionary Society, and with some help from another Christian relief agency TEAR Fund, I managed to organise a placement and was required to have lots of immunisations before travelling including yellow fever and, ironically, smallpox.

I had previously had this vaccination as a child as it was still part of the national programme of vaccinations in the UK in the 1960s, but I received a booster. The irony was that whilst I was away, there was a case of smallpox in Birmingham, my home city, after an accident in a virology laboratory at the medical school, which resulted in the death of a medical photographer, who is recorded as the last person ever to die from the disease.

My journey out there was rather complex, but I had been greatly assisted in planning by the student travel service at the university, who managed to find me the cheapest flights which consisted of changes in Amsterdam, Marrakesh, Sao Paulo and finally arriving in Asuncion, the capital of Paraguay, aboard a Lineas Aéreas Paraguayas plane.

There was one event from the journey I recall apart from the complete exhaustion I felt when I arrived, and it took place in Sao Paulo where I had to change airports. This was by means of a bus journey through the city, which, even at that time, was vast. I had been warned that Brazilian customs were some of the strictest in the world at the time and to make sure that all my documents were in order.

Unfortunately, I dropped my passport at the first airport and did not realise until I had reached the second. Most South American countries use Spanish as their official language, and I had a basic knowledge of this, having studied it at school, but in Brazil, they speak Portuguese, of which I spoke not a single word. I sat next to a businessman on the transatlantic flight, with whom I had had a brief conversation. He was fluent in Portuguese as he worked in Sao Paulo.

During our conversation, I had told him a little about my plans and the reason for my trip. We had parted ways at the airport on arrival, but I was surprised to see him reappear at the second airport. I explained my predicament, and he kindly agreed to contact the first airport. I was relieved to hear that my passport had been handed to the police, and it was now being held by them for me to go and collect it.

My problem was that if I had to return to the first airport, I would miss my connecting flight, and I had no way of contacting the people who were due to meet me in Asuncion. He told me that the police had a policy of not handing passports to anyone other than the owner, but that he would make some more calls to try and sort something out.

To cut a long story short, he somehow managed to persuade the police to give my passport to a member of the airline staff who was leaving for the second airport and who arrived in time for me to catch my connection. I never saw or heard from this man again, who had saved me from a big problem, and I am convinced to this day that he was an angel in disguise!

My return journey was uneventful by comparison, but I did witness two remarkable events—the first was on the bus journey back from the place where I had been working down to the capital. There had been a drought the whole time

I was in Paraguay until a few days before I was due to leave, when there was an enormous storm which caused considerable flash flooding. At the time, most of the Trans-Chaco highway, as it is known, was a dirt road but was subject to considerable traffic in the form of heavy lorries transporting cattle, timber and the like.

This meant that as the road became muddy, great big ruts developed, and the bus actually got stuck at one point, so we all had to get out whilst it was dug out. Later in the journey, there was a shout from a passenger, and the bus screeched to a halt, whereupon he ran out into the bush, whooping and wielding a gun (lots of Paraguayans were cowboys after all), followed by the driver, who had picked up the rifle he kept hidden in a compartment that was used to access the panel displaying the destination of the bus.

These two started shooting into the distance whilst the rest of the passengers, me included, peered nervously out of the windows to see what was going on. They then surrounded a large bush from which they eventually extracted a (live) coati, which is a member of the raccoon family. They tied this up and put it into the luggage compartment—no doubt to be sold on arrival in the capital.

The second event was on the flight from Asuncion to Rio de Janeiro, which was full of Brazilian workers returning from Paraguay. Brazilians are not noted for being reserved individuals, and they are very passionate about Rio—in fact, they have a saying: "In six days, God made the world, the seventh he devoted to Rio de Janeiro," Certainly, it is a city of extraordinary natural beauty. They were clearly excited about returning home as the minute the plane touched the runway upon landing, a huge group of them got up and started dancing Samba-style in the aisle! None of this 'please remain seated until the plane comes to a complete stop' nonsense.

As far as my work experience was concerned, I had a fascinating time. The main health centre was located at a place called Makthlawaiya, which was on a large cattle ranch in the middle of a huge area of tropical and subtropical dry broadleaf forest called the Gran Chaco. This is over 300,000 square miles in size (more than three times the size of the UK) and extends into Argentina and Bolivia as well as Paraguay. Cattle ranching was the main industry in the Paraguayan Chaco, and the ranches were mostly owned by the descendants of the Spanish settlers (often referred to as mestizos) who had intermarried with the indigenous peoples.

Most of the ranch workers were from the indigenous tribes, of which there were three main ones in this area. I have mentioned that Spanish is the main language in most South American countries, but in fact, in Paraguay, the everyday language is Guarani, Spanish only being used for official functions. This, coupled with the three tribal languages in common use, left me somewhat bewildered, although I did pick up some phrases in Guarani. The commonest of the tribal languages was Lengua, and there was an elderly lady who had spent most of her life as a missionary in the region who spoke it fluently. She was much loved by the indigenous people, and they used to say that she spoke it better than anyone else alive.

Much of my time was spent helping to see patients who came to the health centre and particularly in monitoring the tuberculosis patients, especially ensuring that they were taking their medications regularly. We also monitored the growth of the children under 5 years old using World Health Organisation charts and supplemented the diet of those who were malnourished with a locally made, high-protein porridge.

A third project was monitoring the hearts of patients suffering from Chagas disease or South American trypanosomiasis, a chronic parasitic infection that can lead to various complications including damage to the electrical system of the heart. The region where we were working had one of the highest incidences of this disease in the world due to the fact that the insect vector, called the Reduviid or kissing bug, lived in the walls of the traditional huts.

The name kissing bug comes from the fact that they bite mainly at night, and commonly on the cheek of people, whilst they are asleep. The only other insect that I came into close contact with was a venomous spider, known locally as Nandu-pe, meaning 'flat spider'. This was a well-deserved name as they had a habit of hiding in very narrow spaces.

I was leafing through a book one evening in a sitting room with several other people including some of the Paraguayan ranch workers. As I opened a particular page, a spider jumped out from between the pages, whereupon the Paraguayans leapt up and started chasing it with hastily removed flip-flops. I had no idea what was going on, except that I narrowly avoided getting beaten to death by assorted items of footwear. The resulting corpse ended up even flatter than it had been in life.

Our location was very isolated, being about 6 hours by road from the capital and several hours to Concepcion, the nearest significant-sized town. The highlight of the elective for me was taking part in the Annual Measles Vaccination Programme, which involved three vehicles (two of which were Land Rovers, of course) and about ten of us driving to some of the smaller and even more remote cattle ranches to give vaccinations to the children. Measles was still a big killer at the time, especially as many of the children were malnourished and we estimated that each annual trip potentially saved 80 lives.

The roads, if that is what they can be called as they were little more than ill-defined tracks, were often blocked by fallen trees, which necessitated frequent stops to clear the way before proceeding. There were also some suspect wooden bridges which had to be checked for stability before the vehicles were allowed to cross (usually after all the passengers had got out to reduce the weight). It allowed me to appreciate the extent of the Chaco region, although sometimes, the terrain became somewhat monotonous as it was very flat.

There were also numerous large potholes, and on one occasion, I was sitting in the back of the truck with several other people around an oil-drum containing fuel for the journey (no petrol stations!) when we crashed into a large hole and I fell forwards, hitting my face against the edge of the drum. I was wearing glasses at the time, and one of the lenses smashed (being glass, not plastic) and cut my eyebrow quite badly, resulting in my needing sutures from the doctor and a rather unpleasant triple penicillin injection in my bottom from one of the nurses. Unpleasant because we only had glass syringes and re-usable needles which were sterilised after each use, but which tended to be rather blunt. It felt as if there was a barb on the end as well—In fact, I know there was, as the nurse was called Barbara!

One of the missionaries at the base was not much older than me, named Stephen, who was a microbiologist. He had set up a laboratory to allow cultures of tuberculosis to be grown, amongst other projects. We became good friends, and I shared living quarters with him. We used to share the cooking, which was mostly centred, unsurprisingly, around beef, which was incredibly good and incredibly cheap. We had a very limited supply of other ingredients, although onions and tinned tomatoes were available, and we used to try and devise interesting names for our dishes such as 'road traffic accident'.

He has been one of my long-term heroes, although I have since lost touch with him, but I know that he was still working in Paraguay a few years ago and I suspect he is still there. On my journey home, he accompanied me on a brief sightseeing tour to the capital, Asuncion, and the amazing Iguazu waterfalls before I went to Rio for a few days.

Whilst in Asuncion, I had a chance to look at the public hospital and the sole operating theatre for the whole country. I remember it as being very basic and having a wooden floor, rather like something from the Victorian era, but the doctors at the hospital were very proud of it. I also came across a war memorial which consisted of a tank mounted on a concrete pedestal. It was a Bolivian tank that had been captured in the Chaco war in the 1930s. Upon looking at the plaque on the tank, I was amazed to see that it had been made in 1932 at the Elswick works in Newcastle upon Tyne! I had travelled halfway round the world only to find something like that which had been made a few miles from my point of origin.

One of the favours I agreed to do was to take some of the TB cultures back to the UK with me for antibiotic testing as this was not something they had the facilities to do in Paraguay and there were some patients who were not responding to their treatment, most likely due to antibiotic resistance. When I got back to Newcastle and showed them to the microbiologist in charge of the lab, there were some raised eyebrows as to how I had got these into the UK, but once I explained where they had come from, there weren't any more awkward questions, and they kindly agreed to do the necessary testing.

The groundwork for my subsequent career was laid during medical school. We were an ordinary but varied bunch of adolescents trying (and sometimes succeeding) to be grown-up and responsible. Things were very different in those days from how they are now, and some of our worse excesses, I am reluctant to commit to paper, but a few are probably suitable for relating here in order to show you what an uphill struggle training a doctor can be.

I can reassure you, however, that for the most part, the system works as was succinctly demonstrated in our medical school yearbook. This was produced upon our graduation and gave a short paragraph or two about each of the 130-or-so students written by others in the class sometimes with a few prompts from the student themselves. We didn't take ourselves too seriously [who would, when there was a 'nine by nine' club—entry open only to those who had drunk nine pints by nine o'clock (pm I think; needless to say, I was never a member)], and there was even a fictitious student added to the book (I have reproduced the entry with an update from our delayed 40th anniversary reunion below). Sadly, I was unable to attend myself as I have no doubt I would have been able to garner some further memories of embarrassing incidents from the collective consciousness.

MANDY KUYPERS (now FRED)
1980

Mandy originates from Bridlington but spent many of her former years in Port Talbot. She joined us in the fifth year after doing a late C. Med. Sci. in reproductive physiology (she obtained first class honours). Mandy's hobbies

include gardening, knitting, reading, archery, youth hostelling and pony trekking. Her love of animals includes dogs, donkeys and snakes. One of the more adventurous members of our year, she went to Bangkok for her elective.

We hope to see more of Mandy in the future. Good luck.

2022 Mandy underwent a sex change operation in 2012 and is now known as Fred Kuypers.

He returned to the northeast three years ago and can often be seen picking up coal on the beaches of Northumberland.

He has a Staffordshire bull terrier called Gnasher.

The point I am labouring towards is that there were photographs of each of us taken at the time of our entry into medical school—let us say the raw material and then a second one upon graduation—the finished product. The transformation of most of us in five years was truly remarkable! Anyway, back to the examples of our prowess as a group of medical students—one of them includes me, but I am not admitting as to which one. Although our curriculum was modern for its time, our course was still largely divided into the first two years of academic study with lectures on anatomy, physiology, pathology and so on followed by two years of a mix of lectures and clinical work on the wards and a final year of full-time clinical work with gradually increasing levels of responsibility.

This included taking histories from patients, examining them and performing some of the simpler tests. An ECG (heart-tracing) was a good example and combined technical skills (applying the electrodes in the correct way) with clinical knowledge (understanding and interpreting the results). One of our numbers was performing this task on an elderly war veteran with a suspected heart attack and could not understand the resulting tracing—it was certainly not something he had seen in any of his cardiology textbooks.

Eventually, the problem was identified as a failure due to one of the electrodes having been attached to the gentleman's artificial leg—he had had an amputation during the war as a result of injuries sustained! We were constantly being bombarded with the importance of observation as a clinical skill (if you want to see this in action, just watch a few episodes of House M.D.—and yes, I know it is unbelievable, I mean—who would ever be called 'House'?) and I suppose this is an example of how important it is—the ability to recognise a plastic leg as opposed to a real one as you attach an electrode to it.

Another, although perhaps less extreme, example occurred during an orthopaedic clinic with our very vociferous professor of orthopaedics—one of his favourite sayings was "Observation is the neem of the geem"—sorry, but he had a broad Yorkshire accent. He got a group of half a dozen or so Year 4 medical students all looking at the feet of a patient with a foot problem. "What is wrong with this person's feet?" (I have dropped the Yorkshire accent for clarity.) Silence. A repeat of the question with a slightly more urgent tone of voice— more silence. "Just look at them!" Still more silence. This time, the question came with a playful kick to the shins—still no answers were forthcoming despite intense stares from all at the person's feet, so eventually, in exasperation, he told them to count the toes—oh look, he has got twelve!

The third example may possibly be the reason no junior doctors wear a tie anymore (unless it is a bowtie and that needs a certain personality to carry it off.) One of our number was a fan of rather brash ties—if you are old enough, you will remember the type—broad and flowery. He was working in gynaecology at the time and was asked to perform an intimate examination of a female patient (all necessary permissions given by the patient, of course) using a speculum (that is the metal instrument which looks like a duck-billed platypus).

Being somewhat nervous about the encounter, he failed to keep his tie under control (tucking it out of the way between the buttons of your shirt is always a smart move), and unfortunately, as he inserted the speculum, it became trapped inside the patient, and he did not realise this until he tried to straighten up (he was above average height). I think I can leave the rest of the scene to your imagination!

The final one, I will relate for the moment, involved a nun who had been admitted in a serious condition to the medical ward of the teaching hospital where one member of our class (by this time in our final year) was undertaking a locum, i.e., deputising for the ward doctor (in those days called a pre-registration house officer). He had just been checking on this lady and emerged from behind the curtains, which had been drawn around the bed for privacy— this was in the days of the so-called Nightingale wards, where all the beds were arranged in two rows down either side of a large hall-like room—marvellous for supervision and observation of patients, but not so great for dignity and privacy.

Anyway, on his way out, he was met by the Mother Superior who had come to visit, and she enquired as to her well-being. "Oh, she is stable at the moment," came his confident reply, after which he left, whereupon she went inside the curtains to the bedside only to discover that the patient was actually dead. I will return to the Nightingale wards in a future chapter as they always offered the opportunity for unwanted spectacles, overheard conversations and the like.

Later in our course, we started to do clinical placements, which meant spending a period of time (usually between 2 weeks and 2 months) in a particular department in one of the hospitals in the Northern Health Region. At the time, this was the biggest health region in the country and covered Northumberland, Cumbria and Durham. This meant that many of the hospitals to which we were assigned were a considerable distance away from Newcastle, and inevitably, they had a degree more autonomy from the academic centre than did some of the closer ones.

I spent time at two of the furthest-flung hospitals. The first was in Whitehaven where Richard 'Spam' Gatecliff and I spent two weeks doing geriatrics under the supervision of the consultant who was a very enthusiastic geriatrician with a cheery and positive outlook and who always encouraged his elderly patients. At the start of our attachment, he had a brief introductory meeting with the two of us, which he concluded by saying, "Don't get into any trouble, but if you get into debt, I am good for a fiver, but no more and don't get any of the nurses pregnant!" The best part of the attachment from our point of view was that it was a lovely hot summer, and at the weekend, because it wasn't worth going back to Newcastle, we spent most of the time on the beach!

The second fairly remote attachment was in Middlesbrough doing obstetrics and gynaecology at Middlesbrough Maternity hospital. This has since closed down and joins a worrying list of hospitals I have worked at over the years that have either closed or been re-purposed—I can think of at least five. The attitude that seemed fairly prevalent in maternity units at the time was that medical students were rather second-class citizens whose sole purpose was to prevent trainee midwives from getting to secure their required number of deliveries. They were mostly required to sit with the mother to be throughout her labour and, if still present at the end of the labour, assuming all was straightforward, they could then perform the delivery (assuming the mother had agreed of course).

The attitude with which I was confronted, however, was completely the opposite. It was more 'here is a medical student who seems eager to learn and is good company, so let's help him to beat the previous record number of deliveries by a medical student' (somewhere around 50, I believe). Once again, I was resident in the hospital for the 4 weeks of the attachment and, after I had sat with the first couple of mums-to-be and performed the deliveries, I was then just summoned shortly before the birth was imminent rather than having to do all the waiting around.

Because I was willing to be called day or night, the numbers soon clocked up, and I also witnessed these amazing midwives deal with some serious and potentially life-threatening emergencies whilst waiting for the obstetrician to arrive. We were required to write a summary of each delivery in a book to be assessed by the supervising consultant at the end of the attachment. He was a charming man, and by the end of the 4 weeks, I had performed 93 deliveries— more than a lot of midwives get to do during their whole training—and I was awarded a splendid homemade gold rosette by the midwives, saying, "In recognition of work performed above and beyond the call of duty."

I believe I still have it hidden away somewhere. I think they were secretly hoping I would hit the 100 mark, but we seemed to have delivered most of Middlesbrough's pregnant women by that stage. At this point, I would just like to apologise, on the public record, to a lady in Middlesbrough called Simone, who will now be in her mid-40s. Your mother insisted she was going to name you after me before she knew you were a girl!

Having survived medical school relatively unscathed, we were then unleashed on an unsuspecting and trusting public. After completing my obligatory six months each of medicine and surgery as a pre-registration house officer, I was then allowed full rights to practise and started to work as a senior house officer in the accident and emergency department of Newcastle General Hospital (one of those that has since closed). This was where I met my now wife, Lynnette. It was only some while later that I discovered that this was touted as the hospital romance of the time.

When people ask, "Where did you two meet?" they often expect a romantic story, but what they get is, "Over a dead body." Lynnette was a student nurse in the casualty department, and we were attempting to resuscitate someone who had collapsed in the street by doing CPR. Sadly, this was unsuccessful, but it led to our subsequent romance—whether that would have been any comfort to the deceased is debatable. This is not the place to describe our subsequent journey, and I know it would embarrass her for me to include it, anyway, but suffice it to say that we have been happily married now for 38 years.

Chapter 2
Intestinal Gas Revisited

I suppose that as a gastrointestinal surgeon, I should expect most of my professional life to be involved with the basic bodily functions of the digestive tract. Sometimes, this would, however, become somewhat more graphic than I would choose.

I had a very unfortunate patient with Down's Syndrome, whom I shall call Daryl. Not unfortunate because of his genetic disorder—he was a lovely lad— but regrettably, his large intestine no longer functioned properly. He suffered from what we call slow-transit constipation in the trade, but he was at the severe end of the spectrum which meant that, to all intents and purposes, he never managed to go to the toilet to pass a stool himself. Incidentally, the term 'stool' as applied to faeces, which is one of the more polite of many alternative names used in common parlance, appears to have originated from the 16th century when a commode was called a stool.

Anyway, getting back to Daryl, we had tried and failed to get things moving with all the laxatives we had available (quite a lot) as well as enemas which just poured out as quickly as they went in—even the legendary soap and water enema. This particular item ideally needed to be delivered by an expert, and there was no greater expert than the senior nursing sister at the hospital who explained the principles to me in one short, pithy phrase: "high, hot and a hell of a lot!"

I suspect this was the precursor of the now fashionable (in some circles) colonic lavage. I think this was the only time I saw this fail, and he had developed a so-called megacolon, which probably does not require any further explanation. Probably the only thing we did not try was a coffee enema, which is also popular in alternative medicine circles—if you don't believe me, just do a Google search and you will be presented with the 'quality steel coffee enema kit' amongst other items as well as instructions, reported benefits and so on.

Of course, this was featured in the medical comedy TV show 'Green Wing' with a hilarious scene performed by Dr Alan Statham (actor Mark Heap)—a YouTube search will find this for those who are curious.

Often in this situation, we would be talking about surgery to try and improve his quality of life, but neither he, nor his mother, were willing to consider this. The result was that he attended every few weeks for what is euphemistically described on the operating theatre schedule as a 'manual evacuation of faeces'. This was a job that was often assigned to the most junior surgeon on the team, sometimes perceived as a punishment but more often a reminder of exactly what gastrointestinal surgery could involve.

Anyway, being a public-spirited and kindly boss, I often performed the procedure myself and the only specialised piece of surgical equipment required was a dessert spoon aptly, if rather unimaginatively, named 'Daryl's spoon'. It was rather important, however, to ensure that it got careful treatment in the form of sterilisation and was not just shoved back in with the general hospital cutlery after use. It always amazed me just how much faecal material could be stored inside the bowel.

I should explain at this juncture that the hospital I was working in at the time, Bishop Auckland General Hospital, was a rather old one with wards made from Nissen-hut-style buildings all linked by one long corridor running up a gentle slope. Near the bottom of the corridor was the operating theatre separated by two sets of doors. Like all operating theatres, it used what was called a positive pressure ventilation system, which meant that air was continually being pushed out through the doorways to reduce the influx of bacteria etc.

An unfortunate side effect, however, was that this also resulted in unpleasant odours being carried into the main hospital corridor. Often, this was little more than a waft of nose-wrinkling proportions, but when Daryl was undergoing his periodic 'clear-out', it became something more reminiscent of chemical warfare and staff who had seen the procedure listed on the operating schedule were wise enough to retreat into the wards behind closed doors for the hour or so needed for the air to clear.

Fortunately, there was an emergency CPR kit mounted on the wall for any unfortunate hospital visitors who entered the biohazard zone. Having been in the thick of it, I couldn't see what the fuss was about as the corridor air seemed strangely fresh after what I had been inhaling for the previous 30 minutes. There were ongoing debates in the operating theatre about whether it was better to wear one or two masks and risk air trapping inside them or not to wear one at all and get the shock over with at the start before one's olfactory mechanism was so overloaded that your frontal lobe tried to shut it down completely.

As a courtesy to other surgical patients, we tended to perform the procedure as the final case on the list, but I often wondered whether it would have simplified the anaesthetist's role to perform it first—the lingering atmospheric effects aiding the subsequent anaesthetics or even dispensing with the need for one altogether. My major concern was not how many masks to wear but how the smell could permeate a triple layer of surgical gloves and resist extensive hand scrubbing. The only living being pleased to see me in the evenings after these procedures was my pet labrador, Hector, who seemed to find my hands a source of great fascination.

Probably the second smelliest procedure I have been involved with was one we sometimes had to perform during an emergency case when the colon was

 blocked, usually by a tumour in its lower portion. One way of dealing with this is to perform an on-table colonic lavage. This involves washing out the contents of the blocked colon by inserting a catheter into the region of the appendix and then inserting a wide

piece of plastic tubing, generously donated by the anaesthetic department, into the far end (after disconnecting this from the cause of the blockage.)

Often, several litres of fluid are required to do this and, after several attempts of finding a way of minimising the odour, we found that placing the end into a large plastic disposal sac in a bucket which was tied around the end of the tube and then placing a second bag over the bucket and also tying this around the tube was the most effective. This also had the added benefit of preventing the effluent from inadvertently entering one's theatre footwear, which often consisted of ankle-length wellington boots. (Strange how the so-called circulating nurse in theatre was so adept at repositioning the tube!)

After the washout was completed and having removed the blockage, it was then possible to join the ends back together. Since then, however, there has been a move away from this procedure to other methods of dealing with the problem, so I have not needed to resort to this for many years, for which the theatre staff are eternally grateful.

A keen sense of smell does have its uses in medicine, however, as certain medical conditions are associated with characteristic smells. The most important is probably the sweetish odour on the breath of a diabetic patient in a coma due to high blood glucose—this is due to the production of ketones, which are variously described as smelling like pear drops or acetone (as used in nail polish remover).

Nevertheless, a significant proportion of people are unable to detect this, which may possibly be genetically determined. In surgery, the most frequently encountered and much more unpleasant smells are from melaena (the presence of digested blood in faeces) and gangrene. Both of these are sometimes strong enough to be detectable upon entering the ward whilst still some distance from the patient. On the other hand, you will perhaps be surprised to know that pus produced by certain common bacteria is odourless.

Another time when smell is useful is after a patient has had a skin graft. The site of the graft may often be covered by a bulky dressing for the first week or so, and this is left undisturbed whilst it heals. However, if it fails to heal well, there will often be a characteristic smell which can be detected through the dressing. This leads to the practice of sniffing the dressings during ward rounds which always causes a degree of consternation in the patient until you explain why you are doing it and reassure them that it has nothing to do with checking their personal hygiene!

When performing emergency surgery on the abdomen, there are situations when there will be gas present in the abdominal cavity (outside the bowel), and upon opening the abdomen, the smell of this gas can also be informative. For example, it may be from a perforated ulcer (usually odourless) or due to gangrene of the intestine (same smell as for gangrene elsewhere) or due to a perforation in the colon (faecal smell) and so on.

Continuing with the olfactory theme, another occasion when my senses were somewhat overwhelmed was when I was visiting the house of a patient as part of my research project for my thesis (see chapter 5). We were studying activity levels in patients before and after abdominal surgery using a recording device rather like a sophisticated step counter. We were still in pre-smartwatch days, so the equipment was somewhat bulky and complicated to attach. This was fitted to the patient over a 24-hour period at various intervals after their operation following their discharge from the hospital.

The house I was visiting was on an estate in one of the more rundown areas of Newcastle, and from the outside. it appeared to be much the same as all the others. It was a bright spring day, and one of the windows next to the front door was open, and a rather unpleasant odour was emanating from here, which was my only warning of what was to come. The assault my nose received when the door was opened was so awful, I started to retch.

It was somewhat difficult to disguise the fact I wanted to throw up whilst carrying on a conversation, but I did my best and pretended to have a coughing fit. As I entered the house, the level of oppression was raised still further, and I squelched over the soggy carpet in the hallway, pleased not to have needed to remove my shoes as I was led into the front room.

I was invited to take a seat amongst the many cats on the sofa, which also looked somewhat unsavoury, but managed to locate a safer-looking chair with a non-absorbent covering. I have nothing against cats—in fact, I have had them as pets in the past—but when they freely use the house as a toilet and appeared to have been doing so for many months, they can transform it into a highly inhospitable environment.

I politely declined the offer of a cup of tea and set up the equipment as quickly as possible, all the while thinking about my return visit the next day. The patient in question appeared completely oblivious to the situation, and looking back, I wonder whether she was the world's first case of Covid-19. I can understand that you can adapt to a smell, as I used to do when helping Daryl with his constipation, but surely, every time you leave and come back, you have to start to adapt all over again? This was certainly my experience the next day and on the four subsequent visits I made.

The question of the role and value of surgical masks has been debated for many years, and there has generally been a move away from their routine use, particularly in the era of minimally invasive 'keyhole' surgery) I'm sorry, but I must digress once more to give you an interesting but worthless fact about the term 'keyhole surgery', which was actually first coined by the fictional surgeon Sir Lancelot Spratt in the 1954 film, 'Doctor in the House'.

The senior surgeon was marvellously portrayed by James Robertson Justice, and although his character seems extremely brusque and arrogant, I and many of my contemporaries would be able to name several of our mentors who appeared to model themselves on him. The scene in question was a discussion over where to place a surgical incision for an operation. The tentative medical student was asked to draw on the patient's abdomen (with Sir Lancelot having dismissed the patient's anxiety by saying, "Don't worry, this has absolutely nothing to do with you!"). When the student had drawn a small incision, Sir Lancelot grabbed the pen and drew a much larger one, saying, "Too small; keyhole surgery; damnable, couldn't see anything!"

Getting back to surgical masks—whatever the pros and cons regarding patient safety and infection control, there are certainly benefits for the surgeon, as I discovered one day whilst performing an operation for haemorrhoids. This is usually performed in what is called the lithotomy position, where the patient is lying on their back with their legs supported in stirrups or leg supports. The surgeon, by necessity, is in close proximity to the patient's anus, and on this particular occasion, the patient had been given an enema before surgery which had not really done much, especially as the patient had retained a considerable amount of the fluid in his rectum.

About 10 minutes into the procedure, the patient, who had been given a spinal anaesthetic, had a coughing fit. Normally, when you cough, your anal sphincter muscle contracts to prevent any unwanted leakage, but unfortunately, the spinal anaesthetic, in addition to blocking the pain carrying nerves, also affects the ones responsible for muscle contraction, which meant I was the direct recipient of the patient's rectal contents fired in an explosive manner into my face, and that is why I wear a surgical mask (I am also fortunate to wear glasses as I am short-sighted, so I escaped relatively unscathed).

This sort of what one might call 'close encounter of the fourth kind' was not all that unusual. There is a particularly hazardous condition (for both patient and treating doctor) known as sigmoid volvulus. This is where a portion of the lower colon or large intestine twists around, producing a blockage and resulting in abdominal pain and swelling. The first method of treatment is to try and untwist the affected intestine using a colonoscope or sigmoidoscope—these being tubes inserted through the anus. The sigmoidoscope can take the form of a rigid plastic tube, which is disposable and cheap, or a flexible camera, which is neither.

The disadvantage of the rigid version is that it involves peering down the end as it is introduced, thus placing the operator back in the aforementioned proximity to the patients' nether regions. The first sign of success in untwisting the intestine is to be met with a rapidly approaching tsunami of diarrhoea and gas coming down the sigmoidoscope (and often around it also), so one has to develop quick reflexes in order to dodge this before it erupts all over you. This can be a satisfying procedure, however, despite the risk of being pebble-dashed, as it provides immediate relief for the patient who is always very grateful.

The rigid sigmoidoscope was always a much-used instrument in my surgical outpatient clinics as it allowed inspection of the rectum and lower colon and also the taking of biopsy samples where necessary. Most patients accepted the indignity of having a tube inserted where the sun don't shine, but no one imagined it was anything other than uncomfortable and embarrassing—to paraphrase the words of Corporal Jones from Dad's Army (younger readers may search Google for more information), "They don't like it up 'em, Sir."

This was brought home to me forcefully by one gentleman who was unfortunate enough to have a chronic inflammatory condition affecting his rectum which entailed periodic sigmoidoscopies. On this particular day, he asked me, "You're not going to rape me with that tube again, are you, doc?" These days, the flexible sigmoidoscope has become more popular and is perhaps slightly less traumatic.

Since moving to Cambodia, I have continued to see quite a large number of patients suffering from haemorrhoids, and I am not sure whether this is related to the habit of squatting or not. This is adopted as a position of rest by many Khmer people, and it is interesting because most Westerners cannot maintain this position without resting on one's forefeet, whereas Khmer (and other Asian people) can squat with their feet flat on the floor. If you try this yourself, you will probably fall over backwards.

It appears to be because of increased flexibility at the ankle joint allowing the body weight to be shifted further forwards than we Caucasians can manage. Whatever the cause, haemorrhoid surgery has a fearsome reputation for postoperative pain in the early days after surgery (a patient in the UK once told me it felt as if he was passing broken glass when he went to the toilet).

I imagine that using toilet paper exacerbates this as the traditional operation leaves open wounds on the skin surrounding the anus. In Cambodia, however, there is a marvellous device affectionately known as the 'Bum-gun'. This is a small, handheld spray attached by a hose to the water supply and is used instead of toilet paper, so it is also environmentally friendly! If adopted more widely, it would also prevent those insane toilet paper panic-buying episodes of which we have all been critical, but in which we have all secretly taken part.

I think it is a much less traumatic way of cleaning yourself and is especially useful after anal surgery, but it takes a little bit of getting used to after a lifetime of toilet paper, and it took me a while to risk trying it out. I remember having a conversation with my son on this rather delicate topic and asking him about how you dry yourself after using it.

He replied, "Just wave your bum around a bit—it is a hot climate, and you soon dry off!" Maybe this is where the craze of "twerking" came from. The only note of caution I would add is that some of them pack a considerable punch, depending on the water supply pressure, and it can be difficult to control this, leading to some near misses as far as self-inflicted enemas are concerned.

We all know that us Brits tend to have a bit of a fixation on our bowel function, and we are taught from an early age that a high-fibre diet is 'good for your bowels'. Well, it certainly wasn't good for one man who was admitted as an emergency to hospital in severe abdominal pain. He had been having increasing difficulty in going to the toilet, as a result of which, he had resorted to consuming large quantities of bran. He had developed considerable swelling of his abdomen over the subsequent couple of weeks, and then, he had suddenly developed intense pain all over his abdomen.

When we examined him, he was quite clearly suffering from peritonitis, so we took him to the operating theatre and discovered his abdominal cavity was full of the undigested bran as his colon had exploded due to back pressure. He had a cancer in his lower colon which had severely narrowed the lumen (and caused the constipation), and the bran had caused a complete blockage.

It took a considerable amount of washing out the abdominal cavity to get rid of all the bran that had leaked, but after completing this and removing the cancer, he made a slow but steady recovery. Sometimes, other objects can cause a blockage at different points in the intestine. These may be swallowed items (accidental or deliberate) or as part of a person's diet. The latter situation is usually seen when the person has been eating a lot of indigestible vegetable matter.

We had a Cambodian patient a couple of years ago who was admitted with an intestinal obstruction, and what we found in her small intestine resembled a small tree trunk! Often, it is possible to break up the material without opening the intestine to allow its onward passage, but this was far too solid, and we had to remove it through an incision in the bowel. It really did resemble wood, although I am sure it was really a concretion of vegetable matter. The medical term we use for this is a phytobezoar and is closely related to the trichobezoar which is encountered occasionally in patients who are usually suffering from a mental disorder, part of which includes eating their own hair (the human equivalent of the feline fur ball)!

Whilst we are on the subject of the rectum, it would be remiss of me to fail to mention the assortment of foreign objects that are inserted into the anus, and which then sometimes disappear inside, necessitating medical intervention. Such cases have been recorded as far back as the 17th century. All surgeons love to share their examples (with no identifiable details, of course) from lightbulbs to vibrators, but it is rare for the patient to be very forthcoming regarding the circumstances by which they acquired the object.

It is said that the creativity of the person in choosing a particular object is exceeded only by that of the stories they invent to explain their presence. This also extends to vaginal foreign bodies, such as the lady who used to attend the casualty department in Newcastle on occasion, having fallen on the fruit bowl.

Amongst the variety of patients and objects I have encountered over the years, the most unusual was a male patient who was admitted via the emergency department in severe pain due to pressure on his pelvic nerves from a rigid plastic beaker, used normally as a toothbrush holder, inside his rectum. I was called during the night by one of our very experienced trainee surgeons who had spent a considerable time trying to remove this through the patient's anus—initially under sedation and then under a general anaesthetic but without success. My glib reassurance over the phone that 'what goes up must come down' proved to be incorrect, although most of the time, it is possible to retrieve the item in this manner.

There have been many inventive ways described for doing this, but in this case, the object had rotated so that the lip could not be grasped by anything we tried, including obstetric delivery forceps. It was, therefore, necessary to remove this by means of a pelvic operation, which involved opening the rectum from above. However, even then, the beaker was so firmly jammed against the bones of his pelvis that it could not be shifted with any of our surgical instruments.

Racking my brains, I remembered an old gynaecological instrument called a myomectomy screw, which is basically a fancy corkscrew used for removing uterine fibroids. The rigid plastic, however, meant that this would not penetrate the wall of the beaker, and so, I had to use an orthopaedic drill to drill a hole in the side of the beaker first in order to insert the myomectomy screw and pull the object out, which eventually dislodged with a satisfying slurping sound.

Orthopaedic surgeons are rightly obsessional about sterility in their surgery as the insertion of metal plates and so on is always a potential focus for infection, and they were somewhat horrified to discover that a dirty general surgeon had been digging around in someone's rectum with one of their drills! I should reassure you, however, that the said drill was fully sterilisable, and so, there was no actual risk of cross-contamination. Because of the trauma inflicted upon the patient's rectum by the object as well as my rather unorthodox method of removing it, we performed a temporary diverting colostomy until the rectum had healed. The patient made an uncomplicated recovery physically, but there were complications due to the circumstances surrounding the misadventure.

Apparently, his wife had gone out to play Bingo for the evening, and he had gone round to his next-door neighbour who was his mistress, and part of their repertoire involved the insertion of various objects into his anus. On this occasion, it had got lost inside and could not be retrieved by either of them. He was then brought to the hospital, at which point, his wife had no idea of what had been going on. This placed the staff in a difficult position when she enquired as to his condition, because we were unable to explain to his wife without breaking confidentiality.

We therefore referred her back to her husband for him to explain. His version of events was that he had developed serious diarrhoea (apparently very suddenly), necessitating the colostomy. I do not know whether she believed him or not, but I do know, from one of my nursing colleagues who frequented the same pub as the patient, that he used to boast about the whole story to his drinking mates. We closed his colostomy a few weeks later, and I never saw him again, unlike the beaker which sat on the shelf in my office for some years like a prize fighter's trophy. Fortunately, because of the hole, I never accidentally drank from it, but I often wondered about the neighbour's dental hygiene.

Incidentally, whilst on the subject of toothbrushes, a Geordie nurse friend (at a different hospital) once told me how she discovered, as a child, after many months of daily usage, that her older brother had been using her toothbrush to clean his muddy trainers!

Another favourite rectal foreign body is that used by the drug mules who will stuff packs of smuggled drugs wrapped in condoms into their rectums to try and escape detection. I have only seen a couple of such examples, but the important thing is to avoid attempts at removing them, because there are recorded cases of the covering rupturing and resulting in a fatal overdose.

The cases I was involved with were people brought to us by the police who often had been tipped off by person or persons unknown (to me at least), and the uncanny thing was that they seemed to know how many packs there were inside as well as what they contained (usually cocaine—I wonder whether people would be so keen to snort it if they knew where it had been). We would X-ray the patient to confirm the number of packs and then treat them with gentle laxatives to encourage their passage (whilst they were confined to a cell with a commode awaiting the expedited delivery—Amazon Prime, eat your heart out!).

Intestinal parasites are things that tend to make people shudder, but often, they are only apparent by the side effects such as anaemia from chronic loss of blood. The hookworm is a very common parasite in Cambodia, so much so that we tend to administer regular doses of anthelminthic medication to all young children we see in rural areas because running around in bare feet, where there are many stray dogs, and their associated faeces is a high-risk factor. The lifecycle of the hookworm in a human host includes larvae passing from the lungs into the upper airway where it is swallowed and thus enters the intestine.

Sometimes, this leads to a persistent cough, and occasionally, the worms can be coughed up, but the most unpleasant case I encountered was a woman who came asking for medication as a worm had crawled out of her nose during the night!

I find that, over the years, the focus of my work has tended to migrate down the gastrointestinal tract, somewhat like a portion of food gradually being digested. In my earlier years, I spent a lot of time working with oesophageal and stomach problems, but as time has proceeded, I have drifted down towards the colon and rectum. This, perhaps, is an appropriate metaphor for my professional life, and perhaps, retirement will come once I am excreted from the rear end of medical practice!

Going back towards the top of the digestive tract, I recall a lady who was admitted as an emergency case with a sudden onset of severe chest pain. Her description of the events surrounding this was clear enough to allow us to make a confident diagnosis. She was out with some friends at a pizza restaurant when she suddenly felt as if she was going to vomit.

Not wishing to make a scene in public, she suppressed the urge to vomit and rushed to the toilet, whereupon the severe chest pain started. She thought she was having a heart attack because of the severity of the pain, and she collapsed. In fact, she was suffering from a rare condition with the splendid name of Boerhaave's syndrome—in fact, this is the only word I can think of with two consecutives 'a's' apart from aardvark. I am discounting other proper nouns such as Aaron.

This comes from Hermann Boerhaave, a Dutch physician, who first described the condition in 1724. It is caused by a rupture of the lower oesophagus classically induced by forceful vomiting against a closed glottis, resulting in a very high pressure within it. It is a serious condition with an associated risk of mortality, especially if not treated early.

This lady underwent surgery performed by the senior consultant with whom I was working at the time, who was an expert in oesophageal surgery, and during the operation, we found several pieces of pizza within her chest cavity (thick crust, I think) and a hole in her oesophagus, which was duly repaired. Following surgery, she remained very ill for some time due to infection and lung problems, but she gradually improved and was eventually discharged home, suffering no permanent disability. The moral of this story is that it is better to vomit over your friends than to rupture your oesophagus—or perhaps, to eat more slowly.

Sometimes, dietary indiscretions can cause other problems—if they are acute, it is often fairly obvious such as patients suffering from a condition known as Crohn's disease, in which there are often narrowed segments in the small intestine developing an obstruction after eating a bag of peanuts. Other times, the association is less clear.

I remember seeing a young police officer who was suffering from chronic diarrhoea. We had performed various investigations to try and identify the cause, but all the tests came back negative. We even considered laxative abuse, which is a recognised cause, especially in patients with eating disorders, but this was not the case, either. Eventually, we went back to basics and took a careful dietary history, whereupon we discovered that she drank large quantities of Coca-Cola every day at work (6-7 cans).

Once we realised this, we advised her to reduce this significantly, and in fact, she stopped it altogether, and within a week, her diarrhoea had resolved! The moral of this story is that Coca-Cola is better for cleaning the alloy wheels on your car than it is for your health.

Acknowledging the rather strange career choice of colorectal surgeons a comedy due from Canada—Bowser and Blue wrote a marvellous song which they performed at one of the annual meetings of the American Society of Colorectal Surgeons. I have reproduced the lyrics below with the kind permission of George Bowser as they express it much better than I could. If you wish to hear it performed, there are YouTube videos available.

Working Where the Sun Don't Shine
(the colorectal surgeon's song)

We praise the colorectal surgeon
Misunderstood and much maligned.
Slaving away in the heart of darkness
Working where the sun don't shine.

Respect the colorectal surgeon!
It's a calling few would crave.
Lift up your hands and join us
Let's all do the finger-wave.

When it comes to spreading joy
There are many techniques
Some spread joy to the world
Others just spread cheeks.

Some may think the cardiologist
Is their best friend,
But the colorectal surgeon knows
He'll get you in the end.

Why be a colorectal surgeon?
It's one of those mysterious things.
Is it because, in that profession
There are always openings?

When I first met a colorectal surgeon,
He did not quite understand:
I said, "Hey—it's nice to meet you,
But do you mind if we don't shake hands?"

He sailed right through medical school
Because he was a whiz
But he never thought of psychology
When he read 'Passages'.

A doctor he wanted to be,
For golf he loved to play
But this is not quite what he meant
By 'eighteen holes a day'.

Respect the colorectal surgeon
Here and now, we'll raise a glass
For the rectal surgeon, like the rectum
Can tell a liquid from a gas.

We praise the colorectal surgeon
Misunderstood and much maligned
Slaving away in the heart of darkness
Working where the sun don't shine.

words and music by Bowser & Blue
©SOCAN 1996 George Bowser and Richard Elger
Socan # 21893252

My work was summarised in a more graphic way when I was leaving my job in the Isle of Man as I received a cake resembling a pair of buttocks (tastefully covered in pink icing) with a proctoscope protruding from between them—bringing a whole new meaning to the term cakehole. (A proctoscope is a short plastic instrument inserted into the anus for inspecting haemorrhoids and such like.) For some reason, there was also some green stuff around the edge looking more like grass than anything else. I'm not sure what that was meant to represent, but it made a pretty design, and the cake was delicious.

If you are wondering where I got the chapter title from, I have to confess that it is not original. There is an annual scientific conference in the USA called Digestive Diseases week, and it brings together medical professionals working in medical and surgical gastroenterology. It is considered one of the most prestigious and influential meetings in gastroenterology in the world, and I used to try and attend whenever I could. Not only was the programme exceptional, but it was also held in major cities around the USA on a rotation basis and provided an excellent excuse to stay on afterwards for a holiday.

One particular meeting in the 1990s was held in New Orleans, and my wife and I arranged to extend our stay after the conference for some sightseeing and also to meet up with some friends who lived in the same village in County Durham and wanted to explore the area. Simon, the husband, was desperately interested to see what the conference was like—he is the sort of person who takes an interest in everything and who also has an amazing depth of knowledge of many things outside his area of expertise which, at the time, was the manufacture of carbon fibre products.

Officially, only registered delegates were allowed into the conference session, but I managed to smuggle him into an hour-long lecture on the topic of 'intestinal gas revisited'! Despite the rather bizarre title, it was an extremely informative lecture, and I can still recall the main conclusions to this day. My friend also thought it was brilliant and could tick it off his bucket list!

Perhaps, an appropriate ending for this chapter is the sign my daughter saw recently in Bangkok, which she felt should be the name I should use, were I ever to open my own coloproctology clinic!

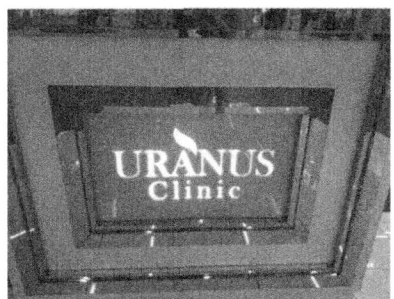

Clinic sign in Bangkok

Chapter 3
Rat Trap

I do hope that most of you readers are old enough to know about all these references I make back to films, bands, TV series and so on. If you don't, then I am sorry, but by way of explanation, the title of this chapter was also a well-known song by the Boomtown Rats, a punk band, in the late 1970s. Their most famous member was, of course, Sir Bob Geldof (he certainly wasn't a Sir at that stage, however) but he rose to prominence and international recognition through Band Aid (the concert, not the sticking plaster) in the 1980s. One of the lines in the song goes, "And pus and grime ooze from its scab crusted sores," which brings me seamlessly onto the topic of arrows (almost).

There is a much-cited picture entitled wound man (see below) which appeared in various European medieval medical manuscripts. In fact, there are

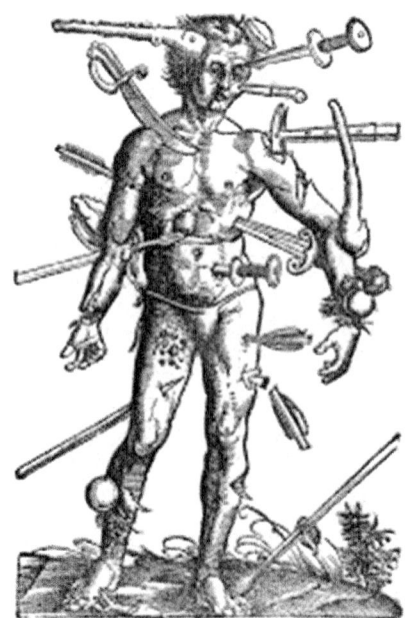

several different ones, but all show similar features, namely a man who has been stabbed, clubbed, speared and shot in a variety of places as well as including other injuries such as thorns, bites and so on. One of these original drawings is now in the Wellcome library in London and dates from 1491.

These images continued to be used for the next couple of centuries. Of particular interest here is the illustration of arrow injuries to his thigh and arm. No doubt these were inflicted mainly during wars, but they are not merely of historical interest—especially here in Cambodia where homemade crossbows and arrows are popular and are often used for rat hunting—hence the title of the chapter.

At this point, I should explain that the Khmer (Cambodian) people are some of the most omnivorous I have met and think nothing of eating delicacies such as deep-fried crickets, spiders, jellyfish, dog and even rats. However, just to be clear, there are certain standards, and no self-respecting Khmer would eat town rats as these eat all sorts of nasty stuff. No, they have to be country rats, where

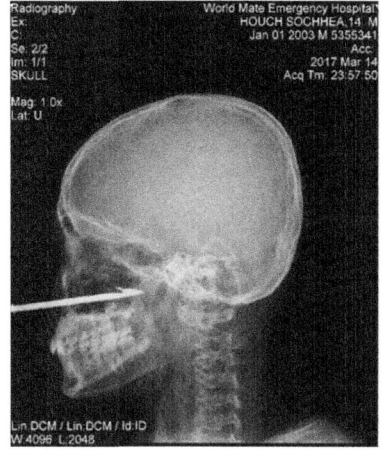

they can frolic through the rice fields and rice mills, eating all the healthy stuff a happy rat needs to grow large and juicy.

Once caught, they are usually served barbecued, having been disembowelled and squashed flat in some way. This results in them looking as if they have been run over by a steam roller with legs splayed and impaled on a stick which, for some reason, always makes me think they look rather surprised.

Of interest here, however, is the technique sometimes used for catching them (usually by young Khmer men) which involves a two-man team. One flushes the rats out (the flusher) and the other shoots them (the shooter). In order to direct the rats towards the shooter, the flusher has to be opposite him.

Unfortunately, the aim of the shooter is not always accurate, or sometimes, the arrows ricochet off the ground and, not uncommonly, hit the flusher. The crossbows seem to be pretty powerful, and the resulting injuries can be serious. I have never heard of anyone actually being killed by one of these arrows, but I have seen some nasty wounds. Two in particular come to mind.

The first was a 14-year-old boy who was unlucky enough to be looking along the concrete drainage pipe containing the rat when his opposite number shot the arrow from the other end, and it bounced off the pipe and hit him in the face between his nose and eye. Amazingly, his eye was unharmed, and the tip of the arrow was embedded in one of his sinuses.

As you can see from the X-ray, these arrows have an unpleasant barb on the end, which makes removal tricky in order to prevent further tissue damage, but he made a complete recovery with no lasting effects. The second case was a little more embarrassing for the patient, as the arrow, which again ricocheted, but on this occasion, went straight into his penis. He came in with his friend supporting the end of the arrow, as every movement was excruciatingly painful, and these arrows are surprisingly long (this one being about 50 cm). Amazingly, it missed his urethra and, having extracted the barb from his scrotum, we were able to cut it off (the barb, not his penis) and remove it. Once again, he made a surprisingly good recovery—he was certainly able to pass urine normally and I hope that he will not suffer any long-term effects.

I mentioned not seeing anyone killed by an arrow, but we did have one rather sad case of a man, who, having broken up with his girlfriend, tried to commit suicide by shooting himself. I am not quite sure how he managed to do this, but from the angle of the arrow, I think he must have put the crossbow on the floor and fired it with his foot somehow. The arrow went in between his ribs, and the tip ended up in his heart.

He survived the journey to the hospital, where the outside part of the arrow (this one was much shorter) could be seen moving with his heartbeat. We took him to the operating theatre and managed to remove the arrow and repair the hole in his heart, and he recovered well. This is certainly the closest I have seen anyone come to dying from an arrow injury and, of course, the circumstances were very different from the others.

Another chest injury was from an arrow which had passed through the patient's T-shirt into his right lung, and he came to the hospital with most of his shirt cut off—just leaving the Nike logo with the embedded arrow—the swoosh as it is sometimes known, which I thought was strangely appropriate...

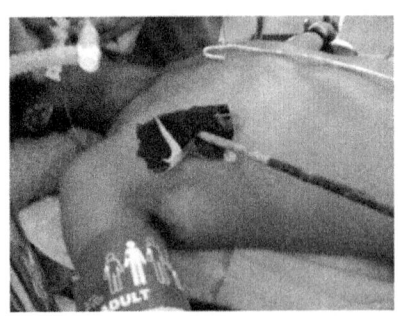

Arrow in chest with Nike Swoosh

Most of the injuries I have seen, both in the UK (and especially on the Isle of Man) and Cambodia have resulted from road traffic accidents, usually motorbike-related, but we sometimes see something a little more unusual.

Fairly recently, a Khmer lady was admitted to the emergency department having been impaled by a cow. She kept a herd of cows and had been bending over to pick something up when one of them for reasons known only to itself, rammed its horn into her rear end. She was in the middle of some fields on her own and had to ride her moto for a considerable distance to get help. I am not sure how she managed to do this without passing out as the entry wound was immediately adjacent to her anus and riding a moto over bumpy roads must have been agony.

The horn had actually penetrated her rectum, and she needed a temporary colostomy after we had repaired the injury, but she made a remarkable recovery and once we had closed the colostomy a few weeks later she had normal bowel function and, in particular, was not incontinent which was a concern I had because the anal sphincter muscles had been damaged.

The other animals that seem to be involved in producing injuries are mainly dogs with occasional monkey bites and some catfish bites—there is quite a lot of fish farming in Cambodia, and I have seen some nasty hand infections following fish bites.

Whenever we see a dog bite, the first questions we tend to ask are, "Was it your dog?" and secondly, "How is the dog?" This isn't because we place more emphasis on the well-being of the dog than the patient, but because rabies is endemic, and if the dog has either died or is behaving erratically, then the patient needs to have post-exposure prophylaxis to prevent them from developing rabies. Unfortunately, I have seen a case of this in a child following a neglected dog bite, and it was extremely distressing to witness.

The mortality rate for established rabies is 100%, but fortunately, there has been a lot of health education in schools and rural communities where stray dogs are rife to emphasise the importance of rabies prevention. Stray dogs are not just a menace in the countryside. There are large numbers in the cities as well and in addition to bites they quite frequently cause accidents by running in front of motos resulting in the driver crashing.

I mentioned the wound man at the start of the chapter and said that his injuries included those produced by thorns as well as weapons. The nearest I have seen to this was a remarkable case of an elderly gentleman who had a nasty discharging wound in his scrotum. He told me that he thought this was related to an accident many years earlier when he had fallen astride a tree stump and impaled himself upon it. At the time, he did not seek any medical help and then forgot about it until it had recently started to discharge. We explored the wound in order to clean it out and were amazed to discover an 8 cm piece of wood inside. That is the second largest splinter I have ever seen.

The largest was, for many years, displayed in the office of the consultant in charge of the accident and emergency department of one of the Newcastle hospitals where I was training (the same one where I met Lynnette.) This was actually a fence post which arrived in the department protruding from the chest of a young man who had crashed into the fence in his car. The consultant, a seemingly dour Scotsman, saved his life by removing it from the patient's heart and repairing the hole it had made.

The patient, who was a member of a notorious Geordie gangster family, was extremely grateful and, before his discharge, told my boss to contact him if he ever had any trouble he needed sorting out! He was one of the most laidback surgeons I have worked with.

He had a large white moustache and a shock of white hair, and he was a chain smoker. When things got fraught, he would usually have a cigarette before

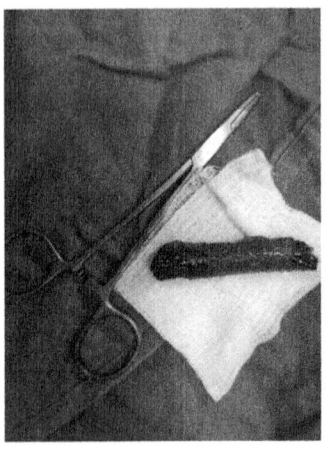

rushing in to do anything. For a while, his senior assistant was a lady who was quite the opposite and used to get very stressed at times—he would always insist she sit down and have a cigarette with him (she did smoke, anyway) before entering the fray.

My friend and I, who were both middle-grade doctors at the time, used to chuckle at the contrast, but it seemed to work well with one balancing the other. From time to time, he used to visit the middle east where he undertook locum

Splinter removed from patient's scrotum

duties and, on one occasion, was faced with the rather unusual request of performing surgery on a Saudi-Arabian racehorse.

The horse needed to have an operation on its thyroid gland, and he did this under local anaesthesia on a very hot day. It was only after the successful completion of the operation that he learnt that the horse was valued at £0.5 million! He told me he was glad he had not known this whilst performing the surgery, but I am not sure it would really have fazed him, anyway.

Another unusual injury again highlights the fact that patients (and their

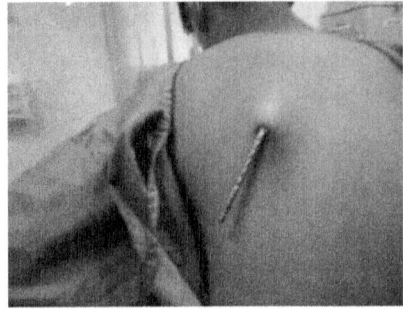

families) do not always tell you the true circumstances surrounding the events leading up to it. This case was a Korean teenager who was visiting Cambodia with his family when he 'fell' onto a metal chopstick which was still protruding from his upper back when he attended the emergency department. Being naturally suspicious, I had visions of the scene in the movie 'Kiss of the Dragon' where Jet Li kills a man with 2 chopsticks to the throat. I could not see how anyone could fall over backwards and land on a chopstick which just happened to be balanced on its end so that the pointy end was facing upwards.

The much more likely explanation was that he had been stabbed with it, although the family stuck to their story. Their primary concern seemed to revolve around evacuating him back to South Korea immediately (with said chopstick still in place). However, as he had a collapsed lung, I managed to convince them that no airline would contemplate transporting him, and they then agreed to allow us to treat him. Ironically, our treatment involved removing the chopstick and stabbing him with a much larger implement, namely a chest tube, to treat his collapsed lung.

"Always remember, the key to victory is not in the size of your army, but in the length of your chopsticks. The longer they are, the farther you can reach for your enemies' snacks."—San Hsu.

If I couldn't have been a surgeon (to my mind, the best possible career in all of medicine), I would have liked to be a forensic pathologist. As I have already mentioned, we had a few lectures in medical school by the home-office pathologist in Newcastle upon Tyne, which were absolutely fascinating, including some of the most gruesome slides of the whole of my training. Unfortunately, in Cambodia, no such person exists, and the police are not often involved unless there is a death or a gun is involved.

Although guns are not a commonly used weapon, knives and other sharp implements are more so. These may be opportunistic weapons that just come to hand during an altercation or something more purposeful.

A few examples which demonstrate the two ends of the spectrum will perhaps suffice here. The first one involved a man who came to the accident and emergency department in one of the UK hospitals at which I was working. He was rather sheepish at first (as well as being somewhat overweight which was probably a good thing under the circumstances) and was reluctant to tell me the story, but he lifted his T-shirt and showed me four little puncture wounds on the side of his waist. These were neatly arranged in a line, and as I was puzzled, I pressed him for more information.

Eventually, he explained that he had been washing the dishes whilst his wife was drying them, but they started to argue about something, and during the argument, his wife got rather carried away and stabbed him with a fork! It was perhaps fortunate that she wasn't drying a knife at the time, as all he needed was a tetanus booster and some reassurance.

At the other extreme was a young Vietnamese woman who was admitted in extremis having been stabbed in the stomach by her husband with a kitchen knife during a more violent argument. The knife had been removed, and it was clear she had ongoing severe internal bleeding, and we had to take her to the operating theatre immediately where we discovered the knife had almost completely severed her pancreas as well as damaging one of the large veins behind it (hence the severe bleeding).

Fortunately, she survived and recovered without any major complications although we had to remove about half of her pancreas. I never heard whether she pressed charges (this was also in the UK), but I suspect she did not, because although the police took an initial statement from me regarding her injuries, they did not follow this up and I was not called to court.

Sometimes, the patient arrives with the knife still protruding from the wound, and in this situation, it is prudent to leave it in place until the patient can be transferred to the operating theatre. I remember one middle-aged lady who came to hospital with a bread knife sticking out of her abdomen. I was surprised to see that one of my non-surgical colleagues was there with her, and it was only later on that I discovered it was his wife, and that sadly, she was an alcoholic who had stabbed herself. She had scars on her abdomen from a previous episode as well. When we explored her abdomen, I was amazed to discover that the knife had completely missed anything important such as her intestine, major vessels and so on, and this was despite considerable internal scar tissue from her previous surgery.

On another occasion, a Cambodian man was stabbed in the chest with a kitchen knife which snapped, leaving the blade inside his chest (see X-ray above). He was short of breath because his left lung had collapsed and, on the X-ray, it looked as if the tip of the knife may have penetrated his heart although, on exploration, this turned out not to be the case. The photograph shows the retrieved blade next to an artery forceps for size comparison (I did not happen to have a ruler with me).

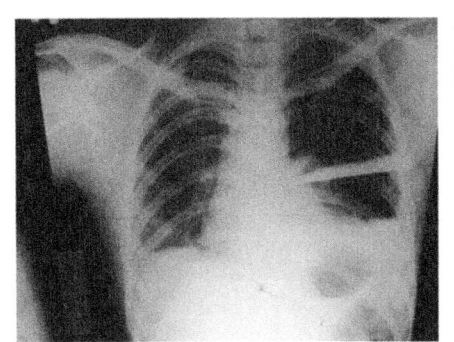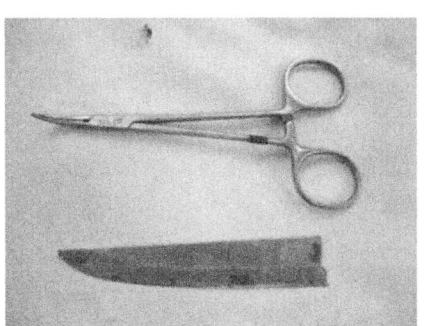

Chapter 4
Accidents Waiting to Happen

When I worked in the UK, I seem to remember a popular pastime was poking fun at some of the sillier items one might list under the general title 'Health and Safety'—whether it be the packet of nuts containing the warning 'May contain peanuts' or the warning 'Do not eat' on the packet of desiccant in moisture-sensitive products. I mean, imagine opening your bottle of paracetamol tablets and thinking, *I don't think these work very well for my headache, so perhaps, I should swallow the little plastic container instead and see whether that is any help*!

However, once I moved to Cambodia where there was little, if any, regulation, I began to realise that there may be some benefits, after all. This view was, of course, brought home to me by the types of accidents we were seeing. Many of these were from building sites, small businesses, in the home and so on and were often life-changing for the victim. To quote the Royal Society for the Prevention of Accidents (RoSPA), "Accidents don't have to happen," and although I am not sure that is entirely true, certainly many can be prevented, and I have seen some positive changes over the last decade, although there is still a long way to go.

By way of background, for those who do not know much about Cambodia or, to use the popular tourist tagline, 'The Kingdom of Wonder' (This has, of course, led to many jokes about Wondering exactly what that means), according to the World Bank, Cambodia currently remains a low middle-income country, and the promising growth in the economy was severely affected by the Covid pandemic from 2020 onwards. The average life expectancy is 68 years for men and 73 years for women. Agriculture (mainly rice), garment manufacturing and tourism are the main sources of income, and although major cities are undergoing rapid expansion and development, the stark contrast between urban and rural life remains.

There also remains some of the long-term effects of the genocide of the Khmer Rouge and subsequent civil conflict, which was only finally resolved in 1998. Some of these effects are attributable to post-traumatic stress disorder and a lingering lack of trust between people, others due to the killing of many academic and professional people by the Khmer Rouge and still others due to the aftermath of war, in particular landmines and unexploded ordinance (UXO). I will return to the latter in due course.

Sugarcane-based drinks are very popular in Cambodia, and everywhere you go, you will see small stalls with a machine for crushing the sugarcane to extract the juice. These are usually run by an electric motor, although some are hand-operated, rather like the old-fashioned mangle which was used to help squeeze excess water out of clothes after washing.

It is, therefore, appropriate to use the word 'mangled' when applied to the wounds created by these machines. Most of them are supplied with a safety guide into which the stems of sugarcane (about the size and shape of bamboo) are placed and fed between the rollers. However, this is commonly removed by the user who feeds the stems through several times to extract as much juice as possible.

The proximity of the person's hand to the rollers can lead to serious consequences if a finger gets trapped. At its most extreme, the entire hand can be stripped down to the bone, and it is difficult to imagine the agonising pain this must cause. I have seen a lot of serious injuries in my time, but personally, I feel these are amongst the worst to witness because I develop a mental image of the accident happening and a realisation that, in many cases, the patient will lose most of the function in their hand, or indeed, the whole hand may need to be amputated.

I have mentioned building sites to be another source of accidents, and one particularly unpleasant type of injury we see is high-voltage electrical burns. This can occur in a number of ways, but one of the more common is accidental contact with high-voltage cables or near contact which, due to the atmospheric conditions of high humidity, can lead to arcing. The problem medically with this type of burn is due to the extreme tissue damage occurring in the muscle, nerves, vessels and other deep tissues along the path of the electrical discharge.

For example, a man was admitted following contact between a live wire and the tool he was using as he swung it over his head. He sustained a burn to his left hand and forearm, and by the time he reached the hospital, there were already signs of loss of blood flow to his hand. Despite performing what is known as a fasciotomy to divide the skin and deeper tissues to release pressure due to swelling, it became clear that all the muscles in his lower forearm had been destroyed as well as the blood supply to his hand.

Regrettably, in this situation there was no alternative but to perform an amputation. Sometimes, it is less clear whether the muscles have been irretrievably damaged, and when making the decision about amputation, I remember the advice I was once given. "If you would buy it as a steak at the butchers, then it is probably OK."

A more unusual case was of a man whose head touched a live cable—I believe he had been wearing a safety helmet at the time, but we only saw him a couple of weeks after the injury—this delay to seeking medical help is common in Cambodia and is due to a variety of factors, which I discuss below. By this stage, he had completely lost the top of his scalp which revealed the underlying skull, and even this had been badly burnt. A large scalp defect like this is difficult to treat, and we had to drill multiple holes in the bone to try and produce a tissue reaction from the bone marrow before we could use skin grafts. We do not have the facilities or skills to perform the sort of complex reconstructive procedures that might otherwise be necessary. Eventually, after several months, it was possible to use skin grafts, which were successful in covering the defect.

Another unusual case was of a man using an angle-grinder with a cutting blade when the disc shattered. Parts of this became embedded in his forehead and, although he was fully conscious, a CT scan which we organised at a private clinic in the city (we do not have our own scanner at the hospital) showed that a piece had entered the frontal lobe of his brain. Clearly, this had to be removed, and because we were unable to retrieve it through the wound, this necessitated a craniotomy which means opening the skull. In fact, it was relatively easy to gain access, and it was removed without triggering any significant bleeding (see photo) and the patient made a good recovery with no dramatic behavioural changes after his accidental lobotomy.

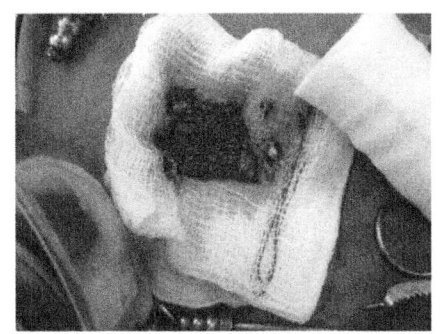

Portion of cutting disc retrieved from patients' brain

Sometimes, patients do display temporary or even permanent changes to their behaviour after head injuries—especially when the frontal lobe has been affected. I remember one incident from many years ago when I was working as a trainee on a six-month neurosurgical attachment in the UK. There had been a crash between a lorry and a tour bus carrying members of a music band following a concert in the city, who were all seriously injured, but one of them in particular had sustained a serious head injury and, whilst recovering, suffered from a period of disinhibition which saw him on one occasion walking down the hospital corridor stark-naked. Fortunately, these effects are often temporary and can completely resolve but are distressing for the family whilst they last. Permanent, but often more subtle, personality changes can occur, however.

Crush injuries are also seen from time to time, for example, a mechanic working on a car which is inadequately supported (often just a trolley jack) and falls onto the person working underneath, most commonly affecting the limbs. Sadly, these injuries are often late in presenting to the hospital as well, because there may not initially be too much to see from the outside, or because the patient will go to the Khmer traditional healers first—a topic I will return to in a later chapter. Sometimes, they will have been treated at a local health clinic which may have not been experienced in treating this type of injury. As a result, we will often see patients with infected or gangrenous wounds, and the only treatment at that stage is often amputation.

Late presentation is a particular problem in Cambodia—sometimes, access to healthcare is limited by financial or geographical difficulties. A few years ago, a patient came with one of the most extraordinary injuries I have ever seen. He came from a long distance away from the hospital and had taken several hours to reach us sitting in a trailer pulled by a moto. The story was that he had been

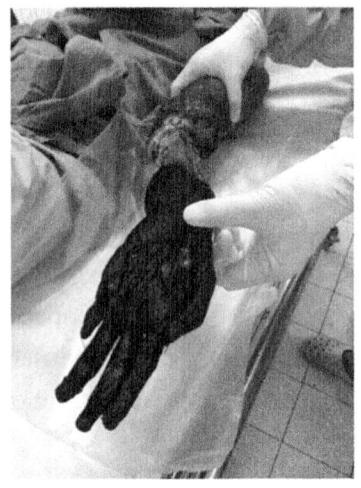

Mummified hand

leading some cows back from their grazing and had a rope which was attached to the nose of one of them. It got a fright and as it pulled away, the end of the rope the cowherd was holding got wrapped around his left forearm just below his elbow and tightened to such a degree that it cut through all the tissue down to the forearm bones.

I am not sure whether he went to a traditional healer, but he came to our hospital several weeks later and asked me whether I could make his hand better. What he showed me was what one can only call a mummified hand—looking like something you would see in a museum of Egyptology in the absence of any blood supply to his hand after the accident the tissues had simply died but had not got infected—merely desiccated.

Obviously, there was no sensation or movement in his hand, and basically, it was just like a simple prosthesis which just got in the way. A useless limb is one indication for an amputation, and we explained that there was no way to reverse the situation and that the only treatment was an amputation but, for some reason, he was unwilling to consider this. He was not getting any pain, although it was tender around the top of the wound, but he left the hospital without further treatment and we never saw him again. For all I know, he may still be walking around with it today.

When I was working as a trainee in orthopaedics in the 1980s in Newcastle upon Tyne, there was what became a high-profile accident at a huge annual fair that is known as the Hoppings. This was first held in 1882 as a temperance festival, and the name came from the fact that dancing or 'hopping', as it was often called at that time, was a part of the festival. It is held every year on the Town Moor, a huge plot of land near the centre of the city jointly managed by Newcastle City Council and the Freemen of the city.

A funfair became an increasingly major part of the event, and it is now said to be one of Europe's largest travelling fairs with up to 300 rides. In keeping with its origins, however, alcohol remains banned at the festival. It is held at the end of June and is visited by over a quarter of a million people each year. It has an admirable safety record for the most part, but in 1984, there was a horrible accident in which a teenage girl slipped out of the safety harness on a ride called the Superloop.

This consists of a carriage within a 20-metre loop which oscillates back and forth, climbing steadily further up each side until it loops the loop, so the carriage is upside down at times during the ride. It was at this point that the girl slipped out and was trapped by her ankle, dangling upside down.

Shortly afterwards, despite her boyfriend desperately trying to hold onto her, she fell to the ground. When she arrived at the hospital, she had severe injuries including to her brain and her leg where she had been trapped. Amazingly, she survived the accident, although she was in the hospital for over nine months. Unfortunately, despite multiple operations, attempts to save her foot were unsuccessful, and she required an amputation, but nevertheless, she adapted well and managed to walk again soon after she had been fitted with a prosthetic leg.

She remained remarkably cheerful and positive throughout her hospital stay, making a good recovery from her brain injury. She became very popular with the hospital staff and probably had one of the longest hospital stays recorded in the orthopaedic department.

On another occasion in Newcastle, we had omitted a rather unsavoury character who had crashed a car that he had just stolen and sustained a life-threatening chest injury in the form of an aortic rupture as well as fractures to his leg. His chest injury was dealt with by a cardiac surgeon, and subsequently, he was transferred to our ward for treatment of his fracture.

He made little of the fact that he had undergone major chest surgery despite a large incision through his breastbone, and we fitted him with an external fixation device to his leg which consisted of a metal bar connecting several metal pins which were drilled into the broken bone above and below the fracture in order to stabilise it.

Despite advice to the contrary, he insisted on walking out of the ward on this and discharging himself shortly after the surgery. When I asked him how he was planning to get home he replied, "I will probably steal another car." At this point,

I rushed out into the hospital car park and moved my own car to a discreet location as the Ford Escort I had at the time was just the sort popular with thieves!

He did return for a follow-up a couple of months later (I didn't ask whether he had driven to the hospital) minus the external fixation device which he had removed himself, and despite everything, the fracture had healed remarkably well. I suspect he had kept the metal pins for use as potential weapons.

I find it remarkable what patients can survive, sometimes despite what we do (or not do) to them. We do not always get things right, but sometimes, things

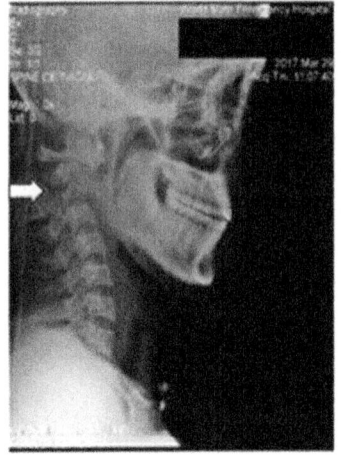

turn out alright, anyway, and, as long as we learn from experience and the patient does not come to any harm, we can move on.

One of the luckiest patients (or perhaps, unluckiest, considering the accident) I have cared for was a teenager who was riding his moto in Battambang behind a trailer carrying a huge load of freshly cut bamboo stems. Exactly what happened next is not entirely clear, but it appears that he collided with the trailer, and one of the bamboo stems impaled him in his neck.

Fortunately, the accident occurred near the hospital. because when he arrived, he had a large laceration in his neck which had actually penetrated his larynx and was partially blocking his airway. We had to perform an emergency tracheostomy to restore his airway and then repair the injuries to his larynx and neck. As a result, he was unable to speak for a few days but seemed to be making a good recovery, although he indicated he was getting a lot of pain from his neck.

We initially attributed this to his serious injury, but the pain seemed to get worse when he sat up and got out of bed. We rather belatedly realised that he had not had an X-ray of his neck and were horrified to discover that he had a dislocation in the upper cervical spine (see X-ray above—the arrow indicates the site of the dislocation)—a potentially life-threatening injury in itself.

We put him into traction, and the dislocation quickly reduced, but we had to keep him on bedrest for several weeks whilst it healed. I am pleased to say he made a remarkably good recovery, but in the rush to sort out his airway, I had overlooked the basic rule to always perform an X-ray of the neck in patients with severe head or neck injuries. It would not have been possible to X-ray him before surgery, but we should have done it once his condition had been stabilised.

One of my early life decisions after starting my surgical training was a result of seeing a patient seriously injured after a motorcycle accident. He was a professional drummer who had such serious injuries to one of his legs that he required a high amputation of one of his legs, which effectively ended his career. I had always been wary of motorcycles, but seeing this convinced me to avoid them altogether.

I have noted over the years that a proportion of motorcyclists adopt a strange mentality following an accident. Rather than dwelling on their injuries or on what caused the accident, they seem to think that because they had survived, they are effectively invincible. They are often more concerned about the condition of their motorbike than themselves, and they have no qualms about getting straight back on to a new motorbike (because the old one had usually been written off) as soon as possible.

One young man who had broken both his forearms in a crash decided that all he had needed was a titanium fairing on his motorbike to prevent a repetition of his injuries in the event of a further crash. This was from someone who had been unable to feed himself or wipe his own bottom for 6 weeks because of his immobilised arms.

It is somewhat ironic that I later spent over 10 years working on the Isle of Man, which is 'motorbike central' with the annual TT and Manx Grand Prix races, which are road races around the island in which motorbikes are driven along the island's roads at speeds of up to 200 mph. There are also no speed restrictions in several places on the islands' roads.

As a result, I saw lots of serious accidents involving motorbikes. Some of them never reached the hospital as they were immediately fatal due to the high speeds involved and the fact that many of the roads are bordered by dry-stone walls. During the TT races, however, there is a helicopter available for immediate evacuation of casualties to the hospital.

The chief medical officer at the time I was working on the island was one of our radiologists, Dr David Stevens, who spent much of his free time involved in workshops and practical training for medics, paramedics and race marshals through Motorsport Medical Services, and he was awarded an MBE in recognition. There was a popular concept around the early management of trauma patients referred to as the 'Golden Hour'—that being the early critical period in which timely medical interventions could greatly improve the outcome for the injured person. He advanced the concept even further and sought to reduce the time for the air-med team to reach the patient down to what he called the 'Platinum 15 minutes' or even the 'Uranium 5 minutes'!

He used to monitor the transfer times for every patient each year, and as I recall, it averaged around 13 minutes because of the 'scoop and run' philosophy. Sometimes, riders experienced horrific crashes and yet escaped with their lives. Two of the most notable which occurred whilst I was working there were a talented local rider who clipped a wall with his shoulder at 160 mph coming off his bike and yet surviving, albeit with extensive injuries, and the second was the well-known TV personality and former TT rider, Guy Martin. He had a crash at a similar speed at Ballagarey Corner (also known as 'Ballascarey' because of the high-speed nature of this section of the course).

His bike hit a wall and exploded in a fireball as he skidded along the road surface, and there is an incredible picture in a video entitled 'TT3D Closer to the Edge' which shows a ball of flame across the whole road with the silhouette of Guy emerging through it. He escaped with surprisingly small injuries in view of what had happened but was hospitalised for a week or so. I remember him as a larger-than-life character; both, physically—he was a big man—and in terms of his personality. He also had the largest mug of tea I have ever seen and as long as he had this in his hand, he was happy.

So, I continued to avoid motorbikes until 2 weeks before moving to Cambodia, whereupon I decided I had better have a basic training in motorcycle proficiency (this was a one-day course to basically teach you how to avoid falling off and what all the controls do). This was because I would need to be able to ride one in what is one of the more dangerous countries for moto accidents, and I had never actually even sat on one before!

In Cambodia, there is little regulation, and you do not actually need a licence to ride a scooter with an engine capacity of 125cc or less, but I subsequently took my motorcycle driving licence so I could use a 250cc dirt bike which was more practical for travelling to some of the remote villages, especially during the rainy season when the dirt roads would become very muddy and treacherous.

The test itself was an interesting experience, comprising a multiple-choice theory section and a practical which merely involved riding round a slalom style course marked with cones, turning a circle and then returning without putting your foot to the ground. The former mainly focused on which vehicles have priority at road junctions with various signs such as 'Stop' or 'Give Way'. This has always amused me as road junctions are a complete free for all with everyone trying to get through at the same time, people coming in on the wrong side of the road and so on.

In addition, traffic lights are considered optional. There were also some questions that had lost something in translation (I think these have since been replaced). One example was, "In which of the following situations should you use your coating lights?" And the most challenging, "How long does it take?" With no indication as to what it was referring to. (The answer, by the way, was 6 minutes!)

There was also a question which basically described a scenario where you were driving along a road and had a choice of swerving off the road with your car full of family members or running over your mother-in-law who was in the middle of the road! No prizes for guessing which was the correct answer; mothers-in-law, it seems, transcend cultural differences.

Helmets (or a lack thereof) are another big issue in Cambodia. Most people wear them only to prevent them from being stopped and fined by the police. Being a bit obsessed with such things, I periodically do a rather unscientific headcount of who is and is not wearing a helmet on a moto, and from my many samples of 100 consecutive riders, the average rate works out at about 50%.

Girls do not like wearing them because it 'messes their hair up' (not as much as crashing and sustaining a head injury does), and many people seem to think that carrying it in the basket on the front of their moto is as good as wearing it. I get particularly frustrated when I see the pupils pouring out of government schools on scooters and motos, many of whom are not wearing them, either. Despite health education on the subject in schools, there appears to be no attempt to actually enforce it.

However, what really gets my goat is seeing foreigners riding without helmets, especially as many of them come from countries where it is a legal requirement (as it is in Cambodia). What kind of message does that send out to the locals? Mind you, at one stage, many years ago, at our own hospital, which was regularly dealing with head injury patients from road accidents, I used to see staff (including doctors) who were still not wearing helmets. I am pleased to say that a blitz on that subject has now resulted in a near 100% compliance rate. As a result of the lack of protection combined with various unsafe practices such as sitting small children in open trailers, I have seen some awful head and facial injuries.

What is remarkable is how well some of these injuries heal. We had a 6-year-old boy who fell out of the back of a trailer onto his face, and who looked as if half his face was missing. His left eye was difficult to identify, and some of the underlying skull was visible.

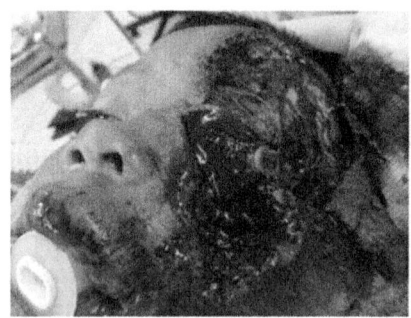 

Severe facial injury   3 weeks later

However, the flap of tissue was still attached and appeared to be pretty much all there. After cleaning it all up and stitching it back in place, it healed really well, and three weeks later, when he came back for review, he had remarkably little scarring and he could see normally. We also had a girl of a similar age whose face was basically split in half but who, once again, had a better-than-expected result.

Road accidents and lack of facilities do not just affect Cambodia. In the late 1980s, my wife and I were on holiday on the island of Rhodes. One morning, there was a crash on the road outside the villa where we were staying. I went outside to investigate and found an 18-year-old man had been knocked off his motorbike and had sustained severe injuries.

My wife and I looked after him as best as we could until the ambulance arrived, thinking that we would be able to at least perform some basic pre-hospital support, but when the ambulance arrived, it was basically a van with a bench for the patient and, although there was an oxygen mask and tubing, there was no oxygen cylinder—or anything else, except for 3 bandages.

The only reason he did not asphyxiate on the journey to the hospital was because I was able to maintain his airway manually. It was to no avail, however, as he died shortly after reaching the hospital. I wrote a letter to the British Medical Journal about my experience as there had been a recent report about the handling of accident and emergency cases around the world. I called it 'Rhodes traffic accident', but unfortunately, they changed that to 'Emergency services in Rhodes'.

No one who has lived, visited or worked in Cambodia is unfamiliar with the horrific period in its recent history of the Khmer Rouge and the genocide that took place during that period. It also left a legacy in the form of millions of landmines and pieces of unexploded ordinance.

I work at a hospital in a town called Battambang (pronounced Battambong) in Northwestern Cambodia. This sits in a large province of the same name, which was also the major centre of operations for the regime after the invasion by the Vietnamese Army at the end of 1978 until it ceased to exist in 1999.

Me next to a Minefield

During this time, huge numbers of landmines had been planted throughout the countryside, and as the political situation stabilised, more land was being opened up to agricultural use, especially as there was massive poverty and malnutrition.

Unfortunately, Cambodia received the unwanted reputation of being one of the most heavily mined countries in the world. This resulted in many people inadvertently triggering the mines which, rather than being designed to kill, are designed to maim (the rationale being that a wounded soldier is more of a burden to your enemy than a dead one).

As a result, there were large numbers of civilian war casualties, and in 1998 an Italian non-governmental organisation (NGO) called 'Emergency' opened a hospital in Battambang to provide medical help for these landmine victims. This work, alongside the efforts of demining organisations such as MAG (Mines Advisory Group) International, CMAC (Cambodian Mine Action Centre), CMAA (Cambodian Mine Action and Victim Assistance Authority) and the HALO trust have saved countless lives and provided care for many injured adults and children, many of whom have lost limbs.

It is estimated that 65,000 people were injured between 1979 and 2022 and of these, over 29,000 were killed (source Landmine and Cluster Munition Monitor). Emergency decided that in 2012, its work was completed in Cambodia as the decline in numbers of landmine victims continued. In 2022, there were only 41 incidents compared with over 1200 in 1998. The government's aim is to be able to declare the country free of landmines by 2030.

I remember being warned shortly after arriving in the country not to leave any marked tracks in the countryside and, if you needed to pee whilst travelling, stay by the roadside! The planned closure of the hospital, however, was stopped when the Handa foundation agreed to take over its running, which it has done ever since. The role of the hospital was expanded to encompass medical services at this time.

Nevertheless, the hospital has continued to see landmine victims over the years with mines sometimes resurfacing in areas formerly thought to be mine-free during the rainy season when flooding affects much of the countryside. Even today, in some parts of the country, a common sight are the red signs warning of the presence of a minefield. We have also dealt with the long-term problems experienced by some amputees who need further surgery for a variety of reasons.

Two examples are firmly fixed in my memory—one not long after I started work in Cambodia as I had never seen a civilian war casualty before. This involved a tractor and trailer carrying several farmers along a track they had used on many previous occasions, but on this day, an antitank mine had resurfaced in the wet weather, and the trailer triggered it, resulting in the death of 4 of the people at the site.

The fifth victim, a young woman, was admitted with extensive leg and trunk injuries, and although she underwent surgery, she sadly died in the hospital a few days later. The second was one of the most distressing cases I have encountered in my whole career: a 4-year-old girl who was playing in a field near her home when she stood on a landmine which destroyed her right leg.

One of the problems with these injuries is the large amount of contamination they are associated with. They frequently contain mud, grass, shrapnel, clothing fragments and so on. I discovered what I initially thought was a stick in the wound, but this turned out to be the remains of her fibula, the smaller bone in the lower leg. We had to perform an amputation at the level of her knee joint as well as dealing with other injuries to her left buttock. This was bad enough, but when she first saw her father after the surgery, she asked him if he could go and find her leg for her in the field.

I found this difficult to deal with on an emotional level, so I can only imagine what her parents were going through. Even writing this now, nine years later, brings tears to my eyes. She made a remarkable physical recovery, and I have not seen her for many years, but one wonders what emotional scars she has been left with. A brief example of the sort of post-traumatic stress patients can suffer from was related to me by a colleague at the hospital who told me that the beautiful hospital garden which had been planted as a peaceful place for patients to sit whilst convalescing had been a mixed success as some patients refused to go there, worried that there might be further landmines under the grass.

It isn't only landmines that cause injuries and, despite education in schools regarding the dangers of handling unidentified metal (and plastic) items, children sometimes do silly things. There is a lot of what is referred to as either unexploded ordinance (UXO) or explosive remnants of war (ERW) still littering the countryside in some areas.

We had a boy admitted with eye and hand injuries. He had been playing catch with his friend using what turned out to be a live hand grenade. His friend, who caught it as it exploded, was killed instantly, whilst he was hit by shrapnel, although at least, he survived. I have also had to extract shrapnel fragments from patients when they are in dangerous places such as the throat.

I realise that these stories are all too often repeated throughout the world and are commonplace in times of war, but they brought home to me that each such episode is a life-changing story for the victim and their families, and they are caught up in a conflict that is none of their making, and sadly, those least responsible are often the worst affected.

The ups and downs of emotions are part of life in medicine, which I think is why many of us develop a rather sick sense of humour. It is one way of dealing with the stress. I would say, however, that at least in my experience, the ups have far outweighed the downs.

Another issue that one has to learn to deal with is the range of cases seen between the serious and the trivial. When I was working in casualty in Newcastle, we did a week of night shifts every so often, but if it was quiet during the night, there was a small room at the end of the department with a camp bed where you could lie down to get some sleep. When another patient arrived, the nurse would come and wake you up to see the patient. Sometimes, this was a little disorientating, and I particularly remember one night hearing a knock on the door with the message, "We have a patient with a spigot in his ear."

As I gradually came to, I had a vivid mental image of someone with this thing sticking out of his ear and wondered why the nurse hadn't just pulled it out for him. When I saw the patient, however, there was nothing protruding from his ear, and it was at this point that I realised I had misheard and he actually had a piece of spaghetti in his ear. *Oh, that is alright then—much less bizarre*, I thought to myself but then wondered, why would someone have spaghetti in their ear? More importantly, was it raw, Al Dente or soft? Did it come with meatballs, or was it spaghetti carbon-ear-a?

In order not to keep you in suspense, I will immediately reveal that it was raw, and he had been using it to scratch his ear canal, whereupon it had, unsurprisingly, broken off. We managed to extract it without too much fuss and then gave the usual lecture on not sticking anything into your ear canals unless it is your elbow.

I don't want to get into a great discussion about creation versus evolution here, but suffice to say that one Christian doctor I have met maintains that one of the strongest anatomical pointers towards the human body being intelligently designed is that your auditory canal is approximately 0.6 centimetres in diameter, and your little finger about twice that, meaning you cannot poke it inside!

I have seen a few interesting things inside ears (and noses, of course, especially in children who seem to take great delight in inserting beads and such like into their nostrils). One of the most interesting was a small spider complete with a web-like nest that had been in situ for several days and must have been tickling like mad.

Chapter 5
The Good, The Bad and The Ugly

I was always told during my training that I should learn from the surgeons I worked with. That meant both learning good habits and avoiding bad ones.

I was fortunate enough to work with a series of talented and experienced surgeons throughout my training. Some of them were colourful characters reminiscent of Sir Lancelot Spratt. These would now be referred to as 'old school' surgeons. One I remember who worked in Birmingham always used to wear a bowtie and looked very smart. He was a very quick surgeon when operating and was critical of anyone assisting him who did not keep pace with him.

On my first day in the operating theatre with him, he asked me where I had come from in my previous job. I replied that I had previously been working in Newcastle upon Tyne, to which he retorted, "I will pay for your return train journey!"

He was very hardworking and expected his staff to be the same. This was in the bad old days when one spent most of one's time in the hospital at work. My contract stated a basic 40-hour week with an additional 64 hours on call. This resulted in little free time for anything except eating and sleeping.

However, every year at the hospital, there was a Christmas charity show put on by the staff. Because of his eccentricities, he was regularly parodied in the show, yet he insisted that his junior staff should be involved in the production of it, and he made sure we had time to attend the rehearsals.

Needless to say, we made fun of him, but he and his family, who were in the audience, loved it. I was involved in several hospital revues over the years, sometimes taking part, sometimes in technical back-up (sound and lighting were my 'thing'). They were always great fun and created a great sense of camaraderie. Sadly, these seem to have largely disappeared with the changes in working patterns.

Whilst working in the same department, I remember a patient who had recently received a kidney transplant. I was asked to see her as she had suddenly become unwell with a low blood pressure and a large swelling at the site of her new kidney. It was clear that she was bleeding from where the artery had been attached, and she needed to be returned to the operating theatre as an emergency. She was in the anaesthetic room, being prepared for this, when the consultant surgeon entered, wearing a pair of surgical gloves.

He grabbed a pair of scissors and had the wound open, the kidney removed, and his fingers on the bleeding artery within 2 minutes whilst the anaesthetist was still trying to keep up. He said, "Here, catch!" and tossed the kidney to an unsuspecting nurse in the corner of the anaesthetic room, who was understandably shocked to be suddenly in possession of it. With this rather unconventional approach, he saved the patient's life.

We had another young woman who had advanced liver damage due to an autoimmune condition where the body's own defences start to attack normal tissues. She came in for a liver transplant, which, in the early 1980s, was only just becoming available in the UK, and I had never been involved in the care of such a patient before. I spent quite a lot of time chatting to her, and she seemed to trust me—she was, of course, very anxious about the whole experience.

The day after the (successful) operation, she asked me if everything had gone well, to which I replied that it had, and that the surgeon had even put a couple of onions in with her liver. She found this hilarious, but unfortunately painful because of her large surgical incision, which hurt when she laughed. I am pleased to say that she made a remarkable recovery, and it was a joy to see her walk out of the hospital after a couple of weeks, because I had previously seen a friend die from the same condition a few years earlier.

Probably the best thing about working on this particular unit, however, was the fact that they had one of these vacuum tube thingies (see my shoe shop fantasy) for transporting blood samples back and forth to the laboratory. In those days, as junior doctors, we took all our own blood samples as there were no phlebotomists and most of the nurses did not do so. Because of the nature of the patients, we were looking after most-needed blood samples checked every day.

As a result, we had large numbers of samples to take and process, and it was great to be able to stick them into the canister and put it into the vacuum system for immediate delivery to the laboratory, some distance away. The results would return by the same means an hour or so later.

We (my fellow senior house officer and I) became quite friendly with the lab staff as we often had to request urgent samples for processing (the transplant unit was given a measure of priority, anyway). On Christmas Eve, I decided to send a different sample, this one a 'urine' sample, which was actually a generous measure of sherry from a bottle, which had been given to the ward staff by a patient. I sent it labelled 'S. Claus—for measurement of alcohol level'. It was well-received by the staff, who fortunately appreciated that it was not urine and sent a Christmas card back.

Being in the operating theatre can be a stressful experience, especially during demanding surgical procedures. This resulted in one senior surgeon undergoing a Jekyll and Hyde transformation. Out of the operating theatre, he was a charming gentleman, but once he entered the theatre, he became a different personality who would shout and lose his temper frequently. He especially hated instruments that were old or not working properly. Rather than let them go to be repaired and then return in a similar state to that in which they had left, he would take them and bend them beyond recognition.

"Try repairing that!" he would say as he tossed them over his shoulder.

He also had an intense dislike of hospital administrators for whom he had a special term, which I will not repeat here. He used to summarise their activities in the following way: "They come here to run the hospital, and after they have made a complete mess of it, they b***er off elsewhere, leaving us to pick up the pieces."

Although throwing instruments is not to be condoned, sometimes instruments inadvertently fall to the floor and, on one occasion, another surgeon I was working with accidentally dropped the scalpel he had been using, which promptly embedded itself in his assistant's toe resulting in a not insignificant injury (not me, I am pleased to say.) On another occasion, I was assisting the same surgeon at an operation. He needed to take a biopsy from the patient's pancreas which contained a mass. This was done using a spring-loaded core biopsy needle, which very rapidly deploys a sharp point which enters the tissue, and then a second part cuts a small segment out, which is retained in the hollow part of the needle as it is withdrawn.

He was holding the pancreas between his thumb and index finger to stabilise it as he took the biopsy and then was manipulating the needle into position before firing it. It was one of those situations where an observer (me) could see exactly what was about to happen, but not in time to warn the person—like seeing someone about to walk into a lamppost, and sure enough, when he fired the needle, the tip entered his index finger, leading to him jumping up and down and emitting a series of expletives and me and the other theatre staff trying hard not to giggle (this, of course, is another benefit of wearing a surgical mask).

A slightly different situation occurred one day when I was performing an appendicectomy. I had recently started wearing (hard) contact lenses as I found them more convenient than glasses, but I had not yet fully adapted to them, and one of the problems I discovered was that a certain, sudden eye movement could dislodge them. Unfortunately, this happened during the operation, and it fell onto the surgical drapes next to the open wound (thank goodness, it did not drop into the wound itself as it would have been very difficult to locate). We managed to rescue it, but I could not reinsert it because of the risk of infection, so I just had to close one eye and finish the operation squinting! The patient came to no harm as a result and, after a period of thorough disinfection, I was able to start using it again.

Another surgeon I greatly admired had a weakness for chocolate cake, and it became customary on a Monday afternoon after completing a long operating list for one of the junior staff to produce a chocolate cake for us all to consume. This was also a very effective way of debriefing after a stressful day's work. This was especially true when we had spent the previous weekend as the on-call emergency team, spending most of the previous 72 hours in the hospital and often working all night.

I later adopted a similar strategy when I was working on the Isle of Man. There was a coffee shop in Douglas town centre called 'Spill the Beans'—a brilliant name, I thought, but also the supplier of some of the best homemade cakes I had ever tasted. (Excepting those made by my wife, of course!)

We were on particularly good terms with the staff as we had treated the lady who did most of the baking as a patient. My favourite was coffee and walnut cake whilst my trusty right-hand man and extremely capable surgeon, Chenji Ratnavel, or Ratna as he was known, preferred their yoghurt cake. So, every Thursday afternoon, after completing our all-day operating lists, we would order some in. This subsequently became easier when the hospital moved to a new building as the coffee shop opened a branch in the hospital foyer. (Nothing to do with us, but a very welcome decision!)

Circumstances in medical training have changed almost beyond recognition over the last few decades, and few people would want to see a return to the insane shifts and working hours we used to deal with. Nevertheless, it induced a certain, almost familial atmosphere in the hospitals, where the junior staff would spend more than half their time in the hospital, and the doctors often lived on site in the doctors' mess.

One particularly onerous job was, in fact, only my second—six months as a pre-registration house officer in medicine at a hospital in Darlington. On paper, the rota did not seem too bad—a 1:4, which means that we were on call one out of every four nights in addition to the basic 40-hour week. So, that meant a 72-hour week (One week is 168 hours. Subtract the 40 hours and divide the rest by 4).

This compared favourably with some of the jobs I would later do such as the one in Birmingham I have described above, which was a 1:2 rota. However, the way the rota worked in Darlington was that each of the four of us was assigned a day of the week for our on-call (to coincide with that of our consultant), and the remaining three days made up the weekend—Friday-Sunday. So, for the unlucky ones (me and a friend called Hugh), who worked every Thursday or Monday, we would be on call continuously, for example, from Friday at 8 am until the following Tuesday at 5 pm—a continuous 104 hours.

It was manageable if things were quiet at night, so that you could get some sleep, but on the occasions when it was busy… I remember Hugh telling me that he had once had auditory hallucinations towards the end of his shift due to sleep deprivation, thinking there was a party going on in his flat whilst trying to get to sleep. (He subsequently chose a career in psychiatry which I always thought was interesting.)

He also informed me that he once threw his pager into the bath in frustration. I did not hallucinate, but I remember reading some of my medical note entries and realising that I had done things like writing the same sentence three times without being aware of it. I also had the rather unnerving experience of being asked on the morning ward round, one day, by the ward sister to countersign a medicine I had prescribed for a patient overnight by phone, but having no recollection whatsoever of having been called.

Another issue was being called to an emergency during meals which we had in the hospital canteen. This seemed to happen with depressing regularity and is, I am sure, the source of my habit of wolfing down food at an unseemly rate. I also blame my bad handwriting on the fact that we had to write copious lecture notes whilst at medical school, because I didn't employ shorthand, and so, I had to write very quickly, leading to a deterioration in my writing (this may or may not be true, but a lot of doctors are noted for their bad handwriting, and I do not recall it being an attribute considered essential for entering medical school). Fortunately, the ward staff were ever vigilant and would pick up any obvious mistakes, but it certainly demonstrates why things needed to change.

It wasn't just surgeons that taught me, however—I have learnt a huge amount from nurses over the years. I was given probably the best piece of advice ever when I was a final-year medical student working on the wards. It came from the junior house officer who told me to always listen to the ward sister and, if in doubt about something, she was usually the first person to ask for advice.

I have mentioned before that final-year medical students were allowed to do locums for the junior house officer (under supervision), and I had the opportunity to cover the annual leave of one of them for two weeks whilst I was working on the professorial surgical unit in Newcastle. The sister in charge of the male ward had a fearsome reputation, being both very experienced and incredibly strict. She could make life very difficult for anyone who got on her wrong side. (And many people did!)

Anyway, I was forever going to her for advice as I had been told to and, as a result, she took me under her wing, and I saw a very different side to her. She was intensely loyal and protective of 'her nurses', as she called them, but displayed the same towards me.

I think she just found the attitude of some of the more arrogant staff (and sadly, academic surgical units seemed to attract them) irritating—especially as her many, many years of experience caring for surgical patients meant that she often knew more than they did, anyway. To find someone who realised this and was willing to tap into it changed her approach completely. Funnily enough, many years later, when I was working as a consultant at another hospital in the region, she came to see me as a patient (she had since retired and moved back to her hometown, but still remembered me).

There was another fearsome sister who ran the operating theatres in the same hospital. I remember her once tearing a strip off one of the consultants in the middle of the ward in front of all the patients (I cannot remember what his misdemeanour was). Whenever I went to see her to book an emergency case, she would say, "What can I do for you, doctor dear?" in a most condescending fashion!

She did run a very efficient set of operating theatres, but I do not recall her ever getting involved in any practical hands-on fashion. The atmosphere between the times she was on and off duty could not have been more different, and I once recall trying to reduce a dislocated hip in a large muscular man. We had placed the patient on the floor of the operating room in an effort to manipulate his hip more effectively, but despite the anaesthetic, I was just not strong enough to manage it. I had called my senior registrar colleague, who had to come in from home, so whilst we waited the anaesthetist, theatre nurses and I all sat around on the operating room floor drinking cups of tea/coffee. Somehow, I do not think we would have done that, had the aforementioned sister been on duty!

There have been other nurses from whom I have learnt a lot. When I started work in Cambodia, there was a senior Khmer nurse who had worked with a lot of overseas doctors over the years and had a huge experience of working with surgical and trauma patients. She was very self-effacing, however (as are many Khmer), and if she had a concern about a patient on a ward round, she would whisper into my ear, "I just have a small question, doctor…"

I quickly learnt to listen carefully to what came next as it would usually be to point out some vital issue regarding the patient, such as the patient with an unexplained low oxygen level after admission with a couple of limb fractures from a moto accident.

"I just have a small question doctor… do you think this could be fat embolism?" (An ill-understood phenomenon when fat particles become lodged in the lungs following fractures.) She continued, "Because when I looked at his conjunctivae (under the eyelids), he had some small areas of bleeding (petechiae)."

This is an often-overlooked sign of precisely that, and she was absolutely correct. She had spent much of her time working with American and other nationalities of overseas surgeons but found my (British) accent hard to deal with, initially. She used to tell me, "When you speak, I hear a lot of air!"

There is also a very senior theatre nurse who has dealt with war wounds for over 20 years. He was helping me in the operating theatre to perform some skin grafts. We use the old-fashioned, hand-operated type of knife (dermatome) to take the grafts—these are adjustable according to the thickness of the graft that you need, and I had not used one for many years. Just as I started, he said, "Do you think that might be set a bit too thin?" His polite way of telling me it was, and so, I let him adjust it for me, and then we got some perfect pieces of skin for the grafts.

This, of course, is the essence of teamwork, and this is never more important than in the operating theatre. For many years, when I worked in the Isle of Man, we had a fantastic team—anaesthetist, theatre nurses, theatre orderlies and so on. Much of our surgery was laparoscopic or minimal access surgery, and the surgeon relied on the assistant holding the camera in order to be able to see what he or she was doing.

As these operations can sometimes take several hours, it requires a special kind of assistant to be able to do this. After time, each member of the team learns the habits and foibles of the others (like one senior scrubbed nurse who was completely obsessional about laying the surgical instruments in perfectly straight lines), and so, it becomes easier to work together. I have performed whole operations where I hardly needed to ask for any instruments because my assistant, Jean Lynch (who was an advanced theatre practitioner), knew exactly what I was going to use next. This reduces fatigue in long operations, and not having to ask for the camera position to be changed constantly also does so.

Another way to help me focus has been to play music in the operating theatre. I have always played background music when studying since high school, so I think this got me into the habit. Unfortunately for the other staff, however, this was not pleasant, soothing classical music or easy listening, as my tastes are more towards heavy rock such as Uriah Heep and electronic dance music, especially trance. The exception to this was in the run-up to Christmas, when we would switch to Cliff Richard singing 'Saviour's Day' and 'Mistletoe and Wine' and other classics like Kirsty McColl and The Pogues with 'Fairytale in New York' and Slade with 'Merry Xmas Everybody'.

One of the theatre nurses had a friend who was the guitarist and vocalist for a punk band called Zero Symphony. She had mentioned to him that I played this sort of music in theatre, and he sent me a copy of their CD entitled 'Break' with a message, "Happy Operating, Mr Stock from Edd!" I have to say, it was a bit extreme, even for my tastes!

I remember seeing exactly the same sort of teamwork as a medical student on my first surgical attachment in Darlington (at the same hospital where I spent my medical job described above). There was a very talented and senior surgeon who worked there and who specialised in oesophageal surgery. In fact, he had designed an operation for oesophageal cancer which now bears his name.

He was approaching retirement at the time I was there but was still busy operating, and he was performing one of his oesophageal cancer operations. I remember the operating theatre was literally full of surgeons visiting from all round the world to see the surgery, and yet, he insisted that my fellow junior medical student colleague and I be right at the front to make sure we could see. He barely spoke to his scrubbed nurse during the operation (which lasted several hours). He needed only to put his hand out, and he received the instrument he required. They had been working together for over twenty years. His technical skills were extraordinary as was his attention to detail. It was this whole experience that was one major factor in my decision to pursue a career in surgery.

Many surgeons display what are known as Type-A personality traits with attributes, such as being work-obsessed, achievement-orientated, stressed, impatient and competitive. A lot of people will interpret this as rather overbearing, although I am not sure this is always the case. (But I would say that, wouldn't I?) Someone once said if you are in a crisis, you want to be with a surgeon because he will make difficult decisions quickly!

Out of all the surgical specialties, I think neurosurgery ranks near the top for stress and difficulty. I met several interesting characters during my six months of training in a neurosurgical unit. One was a diminutive figure who was originally from the Indian subcontinent and who had led a distinguished career including writing a chapter on neurosurgery in a very popular surgical textbook. He was a charming gentleman—more British than the British, and always had time to teach medical students and junior doctors.

He used to tell the story against himself of a time he was at a prestigious medical meeting. Someone was talking to his wife and asked her whether she worked. Her reply was, "Yes, I have a full-time job."

"And what is that?" asked the person, expecting the answer to be something like a neurologist.

In fact, her answer was, "Deflating my husband's ego!"

I worked for another neurosurgeon who was meticulous in the operating theatre, but this also translated into being painfully slow. He would perform an operation to clip an arterial aneurysm (the cause of subarachnoid haemorrhages or 'bleeding on the brain') when they burst and take three and a half hours to do it, whilst one of his colleagues, who was at least as capable, would take one and a half hours. (There was another surgeon who would take just over 30 minutes, but the less said about him, the better.)

The longest operation I was involved in (as assistant, which essentially meant I was peering down the same operating microscope but doing very little helpful) was 17 hours long. One of my predecessors, who subsequently became a professor of surgery and president of the Royal College of Surgeons of England, had a similar experience and summarised it in his discharge letter to the patient's general practitioner by stating, "The tumour was removed cell by cell!"

The two-way communication with general practitioners has always been a vital part of the medical system in the UK, and in Newcastle upon Tyne we were generally blessed with excellent GP's. However, the system did not always work as well as it should have, and there was one GP in particular who would regularly send patients to the accident and emergency department of the local hospital with cursory notes summarising the supposed problem. At its most extreme, this was reduced to a single word, for example, "Heart?" for a patient with a suspected heart attack. His patients thought very highly of him because he would so often get an expert second opinion from the hospital, so they felt they were getting excellent care.

At the hospital, the story was different as many of his referrals were, at best, unnecessary, and at worst, inappropriate. However, he was highly connected politically as well as being a prominent community member, so it was difficult to do anything about it, and no patients came to harm because they were all being assessed by specialists. In fact, one frustrated doctor at the hospital got into trouble for sending a discharge letter back with the "Heart?" patient that merely said, "Heart present."

My own experience was of a 22-year-old woman who was sent by him as a ruptured abdominal aortic aneurysm (a life-threatening emergency that produces crippling abdominal and back pain and swelling often with collapse due to severe internal bleeding). For a start, 22-year-old women do not suffer from this condition, and secondly, she walked into the department with her referral letter which said, "AAA?" Upon taking a clinical history, she said that she was unable to fasten her jeans because of pain in her lower abdomen. Further enquiry revealed that she had symptoms of cystitis due to a urinary infection. The GP had put the abdominal pain together with inability to fasten her jeans due, he supposed, to abdominal swelling to come up with the least likely diagnosis you could imagine.

We surgeons do tend to develop our own way of doing things—not so much surgical operations which tend to be fairly standard unless dealing with an unusual set of circumstances, but regarding the pre and postoperative care of the patient. This might, for example, involve whether we use a surgical drain after a particular operation (a tube inserted through the skin to the site of the operation to remove any fluids that may collect) or how quickly we will start feeding a patient after surgery and so on. This did tend to be more pronounced in the past as in the current era of what we call evidence-based practice, a lot of these matters have been resolved.

One of my early training jobs was on a surgical unit with two senior surgeons who didn't really get on. One was a typical 'old school' type, and the other was the 'new boy' coming in with all his new-fangled ideas. Despite performing the same operations, they did almost everything else differently (almost deliberately, it seemed), which meant we had to remember two sets of instructions and make sure to apply the correct one for whichever surgeon had performed the operation. The interesting thing to note as an outside observer was that it appeared to make no significant difference to the success of the operation as both achieved excellent results.

Another example of low-level interpersonal friction I witnessed was again in academic surgical circles. I was working for an enormously hardworking and talented surgeon who was not lacking in self-confidence. A new lecturer (the academic equivalent of senior trainee) was appointed, who had been working in London, latterly at what he referred to as 'The Hammer House of Horrors', more frequently known as the Hammersmith Hospital. He was a fairly forthright character, which sometimes produced some differences of opinion and led to the consultant saying, "Never trust a man with a Z in his name!" (I hasten to point out this was long before the invention of Facebook/Meta.)

I also remember a conversation between a senior Scottish surgeon and his senior assistant who had performed a gall-bladder operation (this was before laparoscopic surgery had been developed). On the ward round the next day, the consultant asked where the surgical drain was, to be informed that the senior registrar (his assistant) had not used one as the operative field was dry at the end of the operation. This was greeted with the response, "I don't want you experimenting on my patients!"

As I have been a doctor for over 40 years, I have witnessed enormous changes in many areas of medicine, and certainly, this extends to surgery. You have to remember that when I first qualified, the Sinclair series of home computers were still state-of-the-art (with 48K and then a massive 128K; yes, that is right—kilobytes, not megabytes of RAM). There were no mobile phones—we carried radio pagers which bleeped when we were wanted by the hospital (hence their nickname of bleeps) and then had to use a landline to get in touch.

In one hospital I worked in, there was a public address system used to call doctors to different wards and so on—as seen in some of the TV hospital dramas. Most surgeons adapted seamlessly to the many new developments, but a few found it more difficult. One particular example comes to mind of a surgeon who did not trust the new electrical cautery machines used for sealing blood vessels during operations. Prior to this, surgeons would rely on surgical ties with silk or catgut (which has nothing to do with cat's intestines). He saw the advantages, and so, would use it; however, he insisted on standing on a rubber mat when he did so to ensure he did not get electrocuted!

Another area of rapid development has been in the flexible cameras that we use to examine both ends of the digestive tract (endoscopes). When I was in medical school, these were optical. In other words, the image was carried through the instrument by fibreoptic cables, and so, the user had to peer down the end, rather like using a microscope.

My very first boss, after I qualified as a doctor, used these on a regular basis. He always wore a slightly surprised expression, but this was a result of an unfortunate sports accident where he had lost an eye after getting hit by a squash ball. His glass eye was a good match, but a scar had lifted his eyebrow slightly, hence the expression.

He told me that he had been asked about the effect of the accident on his surgical abilities at his job interview (he had only been made a consultant a few weeks before I started to work for him) as there was some concern that his loss of depth perception might be a problem. He informed the panel that it was an advantage when using endoscopes as he had no need to squint by closing his other eye whilst performing the procedure! I was his first pre-registration house officer at Shotley Bridge Hospital (which sadly no longer exists), and I bumped into him shortly after I obtained my own consultant surgeon post, whereupon he congratulated me but told me it made him feel very old to think that his first house officer was now a consultant. (Well, it did take me 14 years!)

Over the years, I have had to operate on several friends and colleagues, which is something I have always found rather stressful as it is more difficult to be objective, something I believe it is helpful to do during surgery. I suppose I should consider it a vote of confidence in my abilities when a colleague asks for help (or more likely, it is just a sign of their desperation). Obviously, there are ethical considerations around friendships with patients, but these have all been people I knew before being involved in their medical care.

One particularly good friend was a remarkable character who has sadly recently passed away at the age of 90 years. He came to me for a routine surgical procedure which passed uneventfully. He was a somewhat eccentric gentleman who had a passion for sport in general but fencing in particular. He founded two organisations, British Veterans Fencing and the European Veterans Association, which continue to thrive, and he continued to fence in his 80s. He won gold medals in his age category on four occasions in the Commonwealth Veterans fencing championships. He was also a keen race walker and table tennis player.

He had lived on the Isle of Man for many years, where he championed schools fencing, and he also ran a small fencing club to which both, the senior theatre sister, Jean, from the hospital and I belonged. He even dragged me off the island to compete in a veteran's competition in the UK, where I proceeded to lose every bout! When the London Olympics were being set up in 2012, Jean and I decided to put his name forward to carry the Olympic torch in the relay across the Isle of Man. He was accepted, and he was so thrilled as this, to him, was the epitome of sport. I felt it was an appropriate way for his lifelong commitment to sport and sporting education to be recognised. He insisted on the photographers taking a picture of him holding the torch with me next to him.

One of the most stressful operations (for both me and the patient) was the one I performed on a medical malpractice lawyer. I had met him several times over the previous couple of years, and he had previously brought his son to see me as a patient. He had also sought my advice on the medical aspects of certain cases he was dealing with. He was a delightful man, although I am not sure I would have wanted to meet him in a courtroom, as he was very sharp-witted.

Because of his line of work, he got to see lots of mistakes and accidents and was very knowledgeable about many aspects of medicine. When his gallstones started to cause him pain, he came to see me, and we both agreed that a conservative course of management (in other words, avoiding surgery) would be the best initial option. Unfortunately, however, he continued to have episodes of severe pain, and we both accepted the inevitable that he would have to have a laparoscopic cholecystectomy to remove his gall-bladder.

He was anxious because he knew all the things that could go wrong, and I was anxious because I also knew all the things that could go wrong and was thinking of the resulting negligence case and the demise of my surgical career! He insisted that I be the one to do the operation, however, so there was no getting out of it.

On the day of the operation, he was almost beside himself with nerves, and as I approached him with the consent form, ready to list in incredible detail all the potential hazards, he didn't want to hear any of it and instead said, "Just give it to me and I'll sign the damned thing!"

This, of course, is exactly the opposite advice he would normally give to anyone undergoing surgery. At least I knew he was fully informed as to the risks. I am pleased to report that all went well with no adverse events, so I am still practising, and he was incredibly grateful.

Another legal professional I had dealings with was the high bailiff of the Isle of Man. This is the most senior judicial position on the island, and the person holding this position is, by law, the coroner for the island. There are some differences between the position of coroner on the Isle of Man (which operates as a crown dependency) and in the UK, but both have the responsibility for holding inquests in certain circumstances to investigate the cause of death.

As doctors, we are required by law to report deaths to the coroner in certain circumstances such as sudden deaths, deaths resulting from injuries and when death may be related to medical treatment. In the Isle of Man, this is normally done through a specially appointed police officer known as the coroner's officer who acts as liaison between the coroner, the deceased's family and any doctors involved in the person's care.

During my time on the island, the high bailiff/coroner was a legal professional but held no medical qualification (as is often the case in the UK), and whenever I reported a case via the coroner's officer, he would call me to ask for further details regarding the case. Being in such a senior judicial position, I was always very deferential towards him, although on the occasions I had to partake in an inquest, he always treated me with the utmost courtesy.

He did, nevertheless, appear to be somewhat austere and, as with my medicolegal lawyer friend above, he also was someone I would not wish to appear before in court as a defendant. On one occasion, the coroner's officer was on annual leave when I called, and I was put through by the police switchboard to his personal phone. I was therefore more than a little taken aback to receive a recorded message from Mr Spock of the Starship Enterprise, asking me to leave a message and something about being beamed up! It just goes to show that our personal and professional lives can be utterly different and may, on occasion, surprise us.

Another example of this was a very eminent professor I worked for early in my career, who was so strict on ward rounds that he insisted everyone leave their bleeps (remember, no mobile phones in those days) in a basket at the nurse's station on the ward. This included the cardiac arrest bleep (although there were other medical personnel in the hospital who also had one of these). He was quiet but firm and utterly professional and very serious, and his discussions often involved several senior consultant colleagues and were, at times, somewhat esoteric. He certainly inspired awe and respect from the junior staff without, in any way, being overbearing.

One weekend, after we had been working for him for several months, he invited all of the junior staff round to his house for an evening meal. This was not really a prospect we relished, but we felt obliged to accept. When we got to his house and met his delightful family, we were amazed at the transformation he had undergone. He was absolutely the life and soul of the party, regaling us with funny stories, playing the perfect host and making us all feel utterly welcome—part of the family in fact. We always viewed him in a different light after that.

I remember, many years later, jointly caring for a patient of his who lived near the hospital I worked at in County Durham. He had written a very eloquent letter, summarising the patient's medical treatment, including the comment, "He is a rather distant character who has some psychological issues and who admits to being prone to depression, no doubt aggravated by spending many hours in a basement playing a computer game called Doom!"

There are a few of my former colleagues with whom I kept in touch after I moved, having built up friendships such as my chocolate cake-loving consultant who sadly had to retire on health grounds and subsequently died of Parkinson's disease. One colleague, however, has been influential in my surgical career more than any other.

His name is Malcolm Clague, a Manxman who was working as a lecturer in surgery in Newcastle on Tyne when I was a final-year medical student. He taught both me and my fellow student on several occasions and offered helpful guidance. He also bucked the trend of most doctors by having the most immaculate writing style I have come across!

I worked with him when I was a surgical registrar a number of years later, during which, he taught me how to perform endoscopies (camera examinations of the digestive tract), and then, he acted as my supervisor when I was doing research for my MD thesis. He actually helped to secure a project grant for the work from the Medical Research Council which, is a coveted form of support from a prestigious organisation.

As he became more senior, he left Newcastle to go and work on the Isle of Man—something he had always said he would do later in his career, and he was a great asset to the healthcare on the island for many years until his retirement, as he was a thoughtful surgeon of great experience. It was through his influence that I ended up on the island myself.

I knew he was working there, and I happened to see an advertisement for a surgeon at the hospital. At the time, there were many changes to the provision of surgical services at the hospital where I was working, and so, I thought I would just find out a little more about the job and sent off for the job description, not really intending to take things any further. The next thing I knew, he was on the phone asking me to come over and have a look around the hospital, the island and so on.

The last time I had visited the island was as a child with my family for a summer holiday (in the late 1960s). Anyway, to cut a long story short, I ended up applying for and getting the job, and I spent the next 11 years there. It was a great privilege to work alongside him as a colleague for many of those years, and he was always available to discuss any difficult clinical issues. I could always blame any of my questionable clinical decisions on him by saying, "Well, you taught me everything I know!" He has been busy in his retirement also, having served as a magistrate for 8 years and becoming the chairman of the Isle of Man Anti-Cancer Association.

Despite my intention to pursue a career outside of academic surgery, I nevertheless spent some considerable time within the academic establishment during my training, doing research for my MD (which is a postgraduate degree in the UK, unlike the American version, which is awarded on graduation) and working in teaching hospitals. In addition to writing up and publishing research, making oral presentations at scientific meetings was another part of the process.

These could be quite stressful events as, after making the presentation, there was time for questions from the floor—often consisting of senior experts, some of whom could be very antagonistic. I never faced questions from him myself, but there was one notable professor who spent his time checking the statistical methods being used in presentations on his pocket calculator and would often criticise or correct the figures being presented.

Medical statistics was always a relatively weak point in many surgeons' knowledge, so it was wise to be prepared in advance. There were some opportunities for humour, however, and I remember making a presentation about some aspect of colonic cancer, during which I showed a slide of a barium enema. Remember, we are still in pre-digital days, so presentations were made using 35 mm photography slides. (A barium enema is an X-ray of the large intestine using a type of X-ray contrast—a liquid emulsion of barium sulphate which was introduced via a tube in the patient's anus—the same technique as those coffee enema fans, I previously mentioned would use, but coffee doesn't show up on X-rays.)

The patient would then be tipped into various positions so that the barium would run round the whole colon. On this occasion, the photographic slide showing the X-ray was unfortunately inserted upside down in the projector (not a problem with digital images of course). As soon as the image went up on the screen, I realised my mistake, but I decided to continue my monologue without interruption, saying, "Note especially our technique of standing the patient on their head in order to help them retain the barium." This did raise some laughs, so I got away with it. Following that, however, I started to use a sticky dot attached to the top left corner of each slide to ensure correct orientation and prevent repetition.

I once attended a lecture in Newcastle by an eminent London professor of surgery, who had a reputation for being a particularly entertaining speaker. He had taught anatomy at King's College, London, for many years. He spoke about good presentation techniques among other things, and he had a slide he had designed which was impossible to project correctly (being a mirror image).

When this was shown on the screen, he feigned ignorance and asked the projectionist if he could turn it the other way up, then back to front and so on before admitting it was designed that way. The point he was making was the importance of checking your visual aids beforehand—pity I hadn't heard his lecture before my own presentation.

With his particular interest in human anatomy, he had gained a huge experience in the causes and treatment of haemorrhoids. When one describes anal problems, it is customary to use a clock face analogy so an abnormality would be described, for example, as being in the 12 o'clock position if it was directly at the top as seen from below with the patient lying on their back. This seems weird, I know, but this is commonly the position the patient is placed in during surgery.

Haemorrhoids are most commonly seen in three positions, and he told the story of how, for many years, he toured the world, lecturing on 'haemorrhoids in the 3 o'clock position', and then, after a number of years when he had completed the tour, did so again, but this time, lecturing on 'haemorrhoids in the 7 o'clock position' and then, finally, 'haemorrhoids in the 11 o'clock position'! There was, of course, a significant degree of hyperbole in this story, but he certainly made an entertaining speaker. Now in his late nineties, he is fondly remembered by generations of medical students and doctors whom he taught.

No discussion of a surgical career would be complete without a reference to the much-feared examinations for the Fellowship of the Royal College of Surgeons (FRCS). These are an essential prerequisite for any surgeon wanting to practise as a consultant in the UK.

The format of the examinations has changed over time, but when I was training, there were two parts—the primary, which was mostly theory and included multiple-choice questions and oral examinations in anatomy, pathology and so on. The examiners in the oral examinations in London (I also took the examination for the Edinburgh college as working in Newcastle near the Scottish border meant that this was largely interchangeable with the London exam) were a pretty scary lot and referred to you only by your candidate number, not your name, whereas in Edinburgh they were a little more approachable and treated you more or less as a human.

This was taken in the first few years of postgraduate training, and the pass rate was very variable but averaged around 30-50%. I failed the first time I took the London primary which was a sobering experience as it was the first exam I had ever failed. I passed the Edinburgh exam, however, and then went back to London for the next set of exams, this time with a little more confidence, and on this occasion, I passed.

The Royal College of Surgeons of England is a grand building in Lincoln's Inn Fields in central London. There is a large lobby with paintings of past presidents hanging on the walls and a large staircase on the left-hand side. This was where the results were announced. The process consisted of the registrar coming into the lobby and reading a list of numbers, having announced, "The following are the numbers of the successful candidates in the primary FRCS examination." Once completed, he departed back into the deeper recesses of the college.

There is a story, which is probably true, that on one occasion, there were no candidates who had passed, and the registrar said his usual, "The following are the numbers of the successful candidates…" followed by a short period of silence before he turned on his heels and departed. Even now, on the rare occasions I visit the college, the memories and associated anxiety come back as I enter the entrance lobby!

The second part or final FRCS exam was taken a few years later and was much more clinically based. This was much more like our day-to-day work as it involved talking to and examining patients (many of whom had interesting physical signs and had been coming back to take part on multiple occasions).

There was also an oral examination on operative surgery. One of my examiners picked a straightforward procedure for me to describe (gall-bladder removal) but was constantly throwing theoretical spanners in the works such as "The patient has now started bleeding from somewhere under the liver. What do you do now?"

I managed to fend off many of these problems, but the solutions I offered did not always solve the problem. "OK, you do that, but the patient is continuing to bleed, and now, the anaesthetist is getting worried because the patient's blood pressure has dropped. What do you do next?"

Eventually, I resorted to answering, "I would call my boss," to which he replied, "Unfortunately, he is on the golf course and cannot be contacted!" Anyway, I passed, so I think the examiner was just enjoying himself at my expense. Having overcome this hurdle, the successful candidates were invited to 'meet the examiners over a glass of sherry' which was almost as stressful as the examination.

Examinations have always been a big part of training in medicine, and I remember vividly my final examination for qualifying as a doctor, which was also heavily reliant on clinical work. Two events stick in my mind particularly.

The first was the patient I had to take a history from and examine as my so-called 'long case'—we were given 40 minutes or so to basically find out all about the patient's health condition and, hopefully, come up with an appropriate diagnosis or a short list of what we call differential diagnoses. The patients had been given instructions before the exams. Most of them were not the 'professional patients' of the surgical exams but merely patients, either on the wards at the time, or who had recently been seen in an outpatient clinic and who had kindly agreed to help out.

One of the instructions was something along the lines of "Don't tell the candidates your diagnosis." The lady I saw obviously took this very seriously, and initially, was very reluctant to tell me anything at all about her symptoms fearing that she would 'give the game away'. I eventually managed to work out her likely diagnosis, but when I said, "You have got Crohn's disease, haven't you?" she refused to confirm it!

The other situation I remember was doing my 'short cases', when you went to see a series of patients accompanied by the examiner, but this time, only spent a few minutes performing a particular examination of one body system. For example, "Listen to this patient's heart and tell me what you can hear."

My one nightmare scenario in the days leading up to the exam was to have the dean of the medical school as one of my examiners. He was a very eminent neurologist, and neurology was not my favourite topic—in fact, at the time, the university had been nicknamed the University of Neurology upon Tyne by Professor Stevens (vide supra) because of the strength and reputation of the department of neurology.

Professor John Walton was his name, and he was a larger-than-life character who used to conduct weekly teaching rounds, in which he would be shown a series of patients in much the same way, except that these people often had incredibly rare neurological diseases. I remember once seeing him write something down on a piece of paper as the patient entered the room and handed it to the co-ordinator of the meeting. He then asked the patients about their symptoms and examined them as one would in an outpatient clinic.

Once he had concluded, he asked various trainees and colleagues in the audience for their opinions, following which he asked the co-ordinator to read out what he had written at the start, which was, of course, the correct diagnosis that he had made within 30 seconds of first seeing the patient!

Imagine my distress, therefore, when he came up to me to conduct this part of the examination. However, he worked hard to put me at my ease, but that did not stop him from asking me searching questions about a patient that I had just examined with a particular neurological problem. As for the FRCS examinations, the successful candidates (nearly everyone, on this occasion) were invited to meet the examiners afterwards (no sherry, though!) and he took the trouble to come up and congratulate me and say, "I was very impressed by your answers regarding the patient with the neurological problem." High praise indeed from one of the foremost neurologists in the country.

He eventually received a knighthood and then became a life peer as Lord Walton of Detchant until his death in 2016. His kind manner, no doubt evolved partly due to his extensive work with children suffering from muscular dystrophy and Newcastle Medical School, thrived under his deanship.

Whilst I was working as a trainee in Stockton-on-Tees in Cleveland, I encountered another eminent doctor—this time, a surgeon whose claims to fame were twofold: firstly, he was one of the first surgeons in the UK to start using a particular type of hernia repair operation which had been popularised at the Shouldice Clinic in Canada, which has performed over 200,000 such operations. He published reports in the 1970s, showing that the operation was very effective in reducing the rate of recurrence of the hernia, which had always been an issue with many of the earlier repairs.

Secondly, he was very involved in introducing and promoting clinical audit as a means to monitoring the outcomes and effectiveness of clinical procedures and was involved in the setting up of the Confidential Enquiry into Perioperative Deaths. (CEPOD). He was later awarded a CBE.

Every Friday afternoon, the hospital held a meeting to discuss these aspects of clinical care, often with a review of case notes from patients who had developed complications after surgery. The trainee doctors were also expected to contribute audit projects of their own. However, not everyone was as enthusiastic about these meetings as he was, and my boss at the time named the meetings, 'Clinical Research and Audit Progress'—or CRAP for short!

Chapter 6
Only in Cambodia

It was Archbishop William Temple who famously said, "When I pray, coincidences occur; when I don't, they don't." The call of my wife and me to Cambodia certainly followed that principle as we had many commitments in the UK that needed to be sorted out before we could leave. To give but one example of many 'coincidences', we were unsure as to what our role would be when we arrived in Battambang, but my ever-resourceful wife had found an advertisement for a general surgeon at what was then known as World Mate Emergency Hospital (subsequently becoming the Handa Medical Centre).

I was to attend a short course in London organised by the Christian Medical Fellowship called the Developing Health Course, which was intended for people like me, going to work abroad in a low-resource setting, to bring us up to speed on a variety of topics such as child health, community-based health, tropical diseases and the like.

It just so happened that Kevin O'Brien, the Director of the Handa Foundation, the organisation taking over the hospital, was in London at exactly the same time (he spent most of his time in Cambodia, Japan and the USA), so we were able to meet up and discuss the job, and he suggested I come and have a look at the hospital as soon as we arrived in Battambang a few weeks later.

I have, for the past few years, kept a photographic record of crazy or amusing

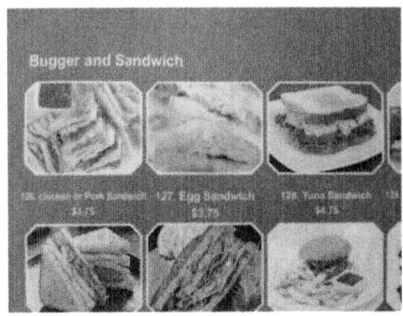

things I have seen here in the 'Kingdom of Wonders'. Many of these having nothing to do with medical matters, and some are related to misspelling or mistranslation of Khmer to English for signs, whilst others are unfortunate names or titles.

One of my favourites shown in the pictures from the menu in a Siem Reap restaurant advertising Bugger and Sandwich. and the sign attached to alternate seats in the cinema after reopening following the Covid pandemic saying, "Please do not shit here." Then, there are the frequently seen toilet instructions including "Do not wash your feet in the toilet," and "Do not stand on the toilet seat." Other bathroom instructions I have seen included "Do not vomit in the sink."

Unfortunate names include the B. A. D. foreign language school, Sor Belly pharmacy and the Il Soon Health Clinic. (The latter was particularly unfortunate as the owner after whom it was named, a Korean doctor, died following a short illness, leading to it's closure.) Another unusual name belonged to one of our hospital outpatients; a Mr Long Nob. Perhaps he had something to do with the restaurant in Battambang called Man Thong!

Sometimes, the translation is less clear. There are a set of instructions in our rented house regarding a card operated power switch which have been 'translated' into English, probably from Chinese, and I have quoted it here. If anyone can work out what this means, I would be delighted to hear from you!

It reads as follows: "NOTICE FOR USE 1. That native checks the electricity invariably in guest room being used dominates. Need thrust when emploing (sic) Ever hear 'Ka Da' voice. 2. When lodger goes out either retreats the house. Pulling out this checks queen, power be able to Yan Shi queen of 20 seconds close down voluntarily." (The two string systems paddles card are not brought Yan Shi.)

I was also surprised to come across a small shop in an even smaller town some miles from Battambang with the proudly displayed title 'Stem Cell Shop'. I have no idea what this is, although I am pretty sure that it is not a state-of-the-art immunological treatment facility. The accompanying Khmer message essentially says, "Your good health is our concern."

The ability of Khmer people to carry extensive loads on their bicycles, motos or trucks never fails to amaze me, and there have been books of photographs published which contain much better pictures than I can obtain.

However, a few particularly amused me—firstly, the man sleeping in a hammock slung across rails on an open trailer being towed by a moto, secondly the people you often see sitting on the top of heavily laden trucks whose job it is to lift any low-slung electrical cables running over roads to prevent them from snagging on the load.

In fact, people will sit virtually anywhere in or on a car or truck, and I have even once or twice seen a man sitting on the bonnet of moving vehicles, not to mention the bucket load of workers sitting in the blade at the front of a bulldozer being given a lift home—not something that seems to bother the police!

Unsurprisingly, we see these people from time to time at the hospital after falling off.

In Cambodia, as in other Southeast Asian countries, fake designer goods are a big business. Sometimes, these are difficult to spot, apart from the price. I bought a pair of Nike Vapourfly trainers for about £12 recently! We also witnessed someone stitching Levi Strauss labels onto pairs of jeans in a market in Bangkok—the same one where I bought the trainers.

Other times, however, the fake origin is easier to spot—the ones I have seen being worn by patients at the hospital include Farari and Nikie sandals, Calvin Kline underpants and a Louis Vutton bag, not to mention items with two different designer labels on them. Because most Khmer people do not read English, I have also seen a number of highly inappropriate and offensive captions on T-shirts being worn by unsuspecting people in the villages. The worst was that of a young woman shown in the photo.

Returning to my medical theme, the third one is something one sees not

infrequently—namely, someone with an intravenous drip mounted on a pole being carried on a moto. I have also seen them being carried on Tuk-Tuks and sticking out of the windows on cars. This needs some explanation, and it relates to the fact that the Khmer place a lot of faith in injections in

Inappropriate T shirt

general and in intravenous fluids in particular.

Clinics and private doctors will insert an IV, give the patient a couple of bottles of fluid and send them home. This is used particularly as a treatment for what is commonly translated as asthenia or fatigue. Of course, Cambodia is a very hot country, and dehydration is an ever-present risk, but rather than advise the patient to drink more, they prefer to use the IV. This service, of course, is chargeable, whereas advice to drink is not, but Khmer people—especially in the rural areas—will often be very disappointed if they do not get one. I have found this repeatedly as I will hardly ever set up an IV outside of the hospital.

IV Drip on Moto

I have been told that the government discourages the use of domiciliary infusions like this, but this seems to have made no impact on actual practice. We also regularly encounter patients who have had home visits from the local doctor and been given injections of who knows what for all sorts of complaints. We do know that steroids play a big part in this, but the patient is never told what they are being injected with.

Cambodian culture is complex and oftentimes mystifying to foreigners (so-called Barangs) like me, even after being engaged in medical practice, especially in rural areas for many years. Of course, I am sure ours is just as strange to them, and it is only when we are removed from our own culture that we begin to realise how it has influenced our lives and thinking.

This is not just my experience; I once met a fully trained anthropologist from the USA who had been married to a Khmer lady for many years and yet admitted that "60% of the time, I have no idea why my wife does the things she does!" To that, my immediate thought was—what, only 60% of the time?

There is a lot of overlap between traditional medicine and Western medicine in Cambodia, and the former also has a lot of spiritual significance for the patient. They will often seek advice from the traditional healer known as the Kru Khmer before coming to the hospital. Presumably, the successes we never see, but regrettably, we see a lot of their failures. This often relates to fractures which remain unhealed and painful after six weeks of treatment. Patients will come to us with traditional bamboo splints under which are all manner of chopped up leaves and herbs and these often damage the skin which delays the timing of surgery even further.

There are also some rather extreme examples of treatment, like the children with diarrhoea who are treated by creating a series of burns on the abdomen (we often see scars on adults, and they look for all the world like cigarette burns). On one occasion, a young girl with a history of mental problems was treated by burning her toes to try and drive the evil spirits out, and she came to the hospital with such bad burns that we had to amputate some of them.

On another occasion, we had a young man come to one of our community clinics with an awful, extensive soft tissue wound to his leg. It had started as a burn when he fell off his moto which landed on his leg, exhaust side down. He had been going to the Kru Khmer for a few weeks with no improvement and it was so badly infected that we admitted him to the hospital.

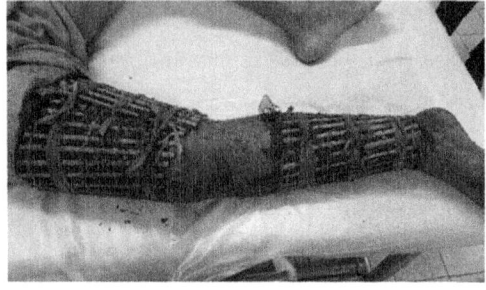
Khmer traditional bamboo splints

Once in the hospital, his leg began to rapidly improve, so much so that we were able to perform a skin graft just 10 days later. It was only when we asked him what treatment he had been receiving that he admitted that part of it was the traditional healer spitting on his wound. Apparently, the saliva of such people is considered to possess special properties.

Concerned that something was lost in translation, I consulted one of our long-standing Khmer friends, who related the tale of religious ceremonies of blessing which he had attended with his family as a child, in which the healer would chant for some time and conclude by taking a drink of water and blowing a big, wet raspberry over the attendees! His rendition of this event, complete with sound effects, left my whole family helpless with laughter, and we have often asked him to repeat the tale.

Sometimes, the family takes the matter into their own hands without any consultation, often with disastrous results. I was asked to visit a diabetic woman at home in one village. I had seen her in the past in our village clinic, but she had developed an ulcer on her foot, and for some reason, the husband felt that applying cow dung to the wound was the best thing. Sadly, this led to an overwhelming infection, and she died before we could get control of the sepsis.

Many people will also use Khmer traditional medicines in the form of plants and herbs, and these themselves may be harmful, especially when used in excess. I recently saw a woman who had been taking large quantities of some herbal remedy and had developed a serious disorder of her nerves, which I think was caused by this. When I first saw her, she was lying on a bed in her house unable to walk or stand and barely able to lift her arms. Once she had stopped the medication, however, she gradually began to improve, and now, I am pleased to say, she can walk unaided and has also regained the use of her arms.

The other type of poisoning we see is due to the consumption of locally produced rice wine. This is typically made by someone in a village in preparation for a wedding or similar celebration and is often consumed in large quantities by many people at the event. Sometimes, due to a lack of knowledge on the part of the person making it (there are licenced producers, but their products are more expensive), it contains an excess of methanol which is highly toxic, and every year, there are cases of people becoming seriously ill and often dying as a result.

On a much lighter note, I was surprised to see a lady walking down the corridor in the hospital a little while ago with half a lime stuck on the end of one of her fingers. Intrigued, I asked her why she had this, and she duly removed it to show me an infected cut on her finger. It must have been very painful because of the acidity of the lime, but she seemed to think it was helping, and it was not the reason she had come to the hospital. Unfortunately, I wasn't able to get a photograph as it looked rather like a lollipop.

It is not just the traditional healers that can cause problems. Although there is supposed to be regulation of the pharmacy trade, in practice, this amounts to almost nothing, and many pharmacists do not appear to have had any formal training. In addition, apart from narcotics and medicines for tuberculosis, HIV and malaria, anyone can buy anything over the counter. Because pharmacies are present in almost all the villages, they are more accessible than some other facilities such as health centres and hospitals. They are also relatively cheap, so many people will go to the pharmacy, describe their symptoms and get some medication.

The problem is that this is often dispensed in small polythene bags containing unlabelled tablets, so if the patient does come to the hospital, it is impossible to determine what they are taking. Unfortunately, it is not just the pharmacies, either, as some of the private clinics do the same and refuse to tell the patient what they are dispensing to prevent them from going elsewhere for their tablets.

There is also a misconception amongst many Khmer people that more is better and to have several different medicines is a sign that the healthcare professional they have seen is really concerned for their welfare. The most extreme example I have seen was the medication given to the parents of a one-year-old baby who had a mild upper respiratory tract infection (aka common cold).

The medication was packaged in various unlabelled bags, and most of this was supposed to be taken five times a day—equating to an incredible 45 doses a day! The only two we could identify were the antibiotic and one other—neither of which was necessary. We have also commonly seen excessive doses of paracetamol being given to children, although fortunately, none of them, to my knowledge, have come to any serious harm.

Another thing I have seen is the pharmacy providing a small bag of sugar to go with the tablets—perhaps they had just been to see Mary Poppins. Lack of regulation in healthcare is a big problem in Cambodia, although in recent years, the government has been starting to tighten things up, and several clinics offering cosmetic treatment have been shut down recently due to unlicenced practitioners giving treatment.

There was a tragic case in 2014 of a 'doctor' working in one of the villages near where I live, who was reusing needles to give injections. In fact, he had no medical degree and, having used a needle on a patient with undiagnosed HIV, he then created an epidemic of cases, totalling 242 people out of 2000 in the village.

98% of these were infected with the same strain of the virus. Approximately 80% were also infected with Hepatitis C, which was thought to have started from three different sources of contamination a few months earlier. The age range was from 2 to 89 years and included some of his own family. The individual responsible was arrested and is now serving a 25-year sentence in prison.

Corruption is a big problem, and I have personally witnessed many cases where medical advice is given based on financial factors and not health benefits. In fact, I spend a significant proportion of my time at the hospital dissuading people from undergoing surgery that they have been told they should have. For example, removing small ovarian cysts that are causing no symptoms or removing part of the large intestine for tiny, benign polyps. This is because private clinics make more money from operating on people than merely offering advice.

Fortunately, some of the patients come to us for a second opinion before committing to surgery. One of the worst examples I have seen was of an obstetrician who performed prenatal scans for pregnant women and then falsified the expected date of delivery to one month before the baby was actually due. He then told the women that if they had not delivered the baby by two weeks after the (false) date, they should come to his clinic for a Caesarean section. This meant that he could charge for what was clearly an unnecessary procedure as, at this point, the baby was not due for a further two weeks.

Another scenario we often see is over-investigation. This is sometimes driven by the patient who, for example, will go and get three ultrasound scans at different clinics because they do not trust any one individual to get it right. It can also, however, be another way of clinics generating income. I recently saw a boy with calluses on his feet who had undergone an X-ray followed by a CT scan. The latter was of such poor quality that it gave less information than the X-ray, and it was unnecessary, anyway.

Another patient came to see me at the hospital with a small lump on their arm, which was quite clearly what we call a lipoma—this being a collection of fatty cells that form into a swelling. They are common, easily diagnosed and completely harmless. The patient brought with them the ultrasound, CT scan and MRI scan they had undergone for this! None of these were necessary, let alone all three, and it would have cost the patient at least two hundred and fifty pounds—money many Khmer can ill-afford to spend.

Lack of training is also an issue—my wife quotes the expression 'All the gear and no idea'. In other words, it is no use having all the high-tech equipment if you do not know how to use it. We recently sent a man for a CT scan of his abdomen to one of the large private clinics in town (we do not have our own CT scanner). He had a large mass we could feel, and I suspected a cancer involving the soft tissues at the back of his abdomen. The report came back saying in summary, 'Advanced ovarian cancer, uterus normal'!

We also see some interesting investigations being performed by unscrupulous individuals who go around villages offering free tests of various kinds, which then lead to a series of results ostensibly indicating the need for medication which, of course, is available from the company they represent—at a price.

I have managed to get my hands on a couple of these reports and some of the more extraordinary tests include those measured by the quantum resonance magnetic analyser such as 'Small intestine peristalsis function coefficient', 'Left ventricular effective pump power' and 'Prostatitis syndrome'. This is a handheld device that is said to function by measuring the body's magnetic field and is said to be able to assess 35 or so different parameters including blood glucose although testing this last claim has shown it to be wholly ineffective.

Interestingly, all the reference ranges use only numbers with no units of measurement and, as there is no means of comparing the results with other methods of measurement, the results are meaningless. Another series of tests a patient brought to one of the rural clinics showed a grid of boxes with organs listed down one side (including anatomical structures such as head, left arm etc. as well as organs) and symptoms along the top. There were ticks in various boxes showing the patient had, amongst other things, mercury in the right lung, deficiency of the head, toxin in the left leg, etc. Sadly, taking advantage of people with no medical knowledge or understanding is commonplace.

Late presentation of illness is something I have already mentioned, and although this is not exclusive to Cambodia, it is a common problem, as I have already alluded. This, coupled with the stoicism of many Khmer people, can produce some gross examples of disease processes or what one of my past bosses would refer to as 'Gothic Horrors'.

Last year, we saw a middle-aged lady in our surgical clinic with pain in her left breast. She had been putting up with this for several weeks, and when we examined her, we noted the left breast was approximately twice the size of the right one with clear signs of an underlying abscess. When we took her to the operating theatre to drain this, the pus just kept coming and coming. In fact, we drained 1300 ml from it. She must have been in agony but made relatively little of it, but over the years, I have come to realise that the things I was used to seeing in the UK do not apply here in Cambodia.

Gone are the assumptions that people who walk into the emergency room complaining of abdominal pain are unlikely to have appendicitis. In fact, I have rarely seen anyone with appendicitis *not* walk in. I have also seen some patients with more serious problems like peritonitis do the same. At the other end of the spectrum, however, we see people who will faint whilst having blood samples taken, and this often seems to be the young men with multiple tattoos which has always puzzled me—if they do not like needles, why do they get tattoos? Interestingly, this is something I used to see in the UK as well.

One of the first cases I saw when I arrived in Cambodia was a 13-year-old girl who was brought to the hospital by her father because she could not move her elbow. She had a history of having fallen out of a tree eight months earlier and had been to the traditional healer thereafter, but not sought medical help.

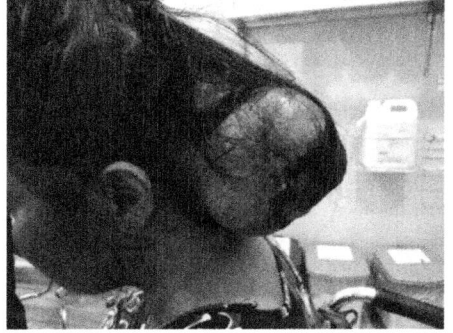 Examining her I was shocked to discover that her elbow was dislocated, and X-rays confirmed that this was indeed long-standing.

I also saw a lady a couple of years ago who had a huge tumour on the back of her head (see photo) which was so big it was approaching the size of her head. It was difficult to know what sort of tumour this was, although an X-ray clearly showed that it had destroyed the posterior part of her skull. Apart from the sheer size of it, she denied any symptoms, and in particular, no sign of any neurological problems. She wanted us to remove it for her, but unfortunately, it was way beyond our capabilities to do that.

Another lady I saw with a late presentation of a breast problem was a lady who had put up with a smelly, discharging ulcer on her breast for about three years. This had been steadily increasing in size, and eventually, she sought help. When I examined her, the whole of her breast was involved with a huge, ulcerated breast cancer. Closer inspection revealed the presence of maggots within it, which were busy feeding on the dead tissue. We performed what is often referred to as a toilet mastectomy, which is basically to remove the tumour in order to relieve some of the patient's symptoms, although it was clear that we were not going to be able to cure her.

Unfortunately, the cost and limited availability of additional treatments such as radiotherapy and chemotherapy make these beyond the reach of many of the patients we see.

Closer to home, another group of people who seem to be particularly stoical are farmers. When I worked in Bishop Auckland, our catchment population included farmers from some of the more remote parts of the north of England such as Weardale, Teesdale and the Pennines. These hardy folk were busy the year round and had little spare time to visit doctors, unless there was some major problem, so I always took their concerns particularly seriously.

I once had the wife of a farmer in her 40s who lived out in the hills beyond Stanhope who came to see me, saying that she was having a bit of bother with haemorrhoids, and she found it uncomfortable to sit down. When I examined her, I was horrified to find a huge cancer protruding through her anus and involving her vagina, producing a connection between them (a fistula). She claimed to have only been experiencing symptoms for a couple of weeks, but I found that very hard to believe. Regrettably, despite treatment, she eventually succumbed to the disease.

One of the challenges of working in a lower-middle-income country is that many of the pieces of equipment we would like to have are either too expensive or not available at all. Occasionally, one is caught in a situation where there is just no access to anything. One time, I was at a remote location where a small conference was being held. One of the conference attendees was a young woman who had a bite on her calf which had become infected and turned into an abscess (this particular type of bite also tended to develop a lump of fairly solid, dead material which needs to be removed in order to allow the abscess to drain).

I had absolutely no equipment, but she was in so much pain that we had to improvise. This consisted of an ice pack applied for 5 minutes as an anaesthetic, some soap as antiseptic and a kitchen knife (rather blunt) for scalpel. She was very uncomplaining, although I am sure it was a thoroughly unpleasant experience for her. Interestingly, as I write this, I am listening to 'Comfortably Numb' by Pink Floyd—pure coincidence.

Many years earlier, in Bishop Auckland, when my children were young, my daughter had a friend around to play who fell and cut her leg quite badly. I used to keep a set of minor surgical instruments at home as well as some sutures and local anaesthetic, and she agreed to my stitching the wound at home rather than having to take her all the way to the hospital (where I would have undertaken the necessary procedure, anyway), so we laid her on the best surface we could find—our very large kitchen table and stitched her wound up—my wife, being a trained nurse, assisting me.

Sometimes, one can improvise, and we devised a simple solution for creating a device called a spacer. This is a device which makes it easier for children (and adults) to use an inhaler. It is normally a plastic tube of some sort with an attachment on one end for the inhaler and a mouthpiece on the other end for the patient to breathe through. I doubt our idea was original, but we discovered that a simple disposable plastic cup was ideal as you can cut a suitable shaped hole in the bottom for the inhaler, and the open-end fits quite well over a toddler's mouth and nose. These cups are ubiquitous in Cambodia, so once the parent has been shown what to do, they can make further ones as they are not very sturdy and can only be used a few times each.

Plastic cup spacer in use

Returning to the subject of old-fashioned equipment, when I first arrived in Cambodia, the drill we used for drilling holes in the skull for the emergency treatment of blood clots on the brain following head injuries was a hand-operated brace and bit instrument called a Hudson brace. These are still used around the world, but ours was rather old and somewhat blunt, and I always felt I had to 'brace myself before it bit'.

In fact, considering the delicacy of neurosurgery in general, the whole procedure was rather brutal—first you had to drill a series of holes through the skull on the affected side using just the right amount of pressure to cut through the bone without suddenly penetrating the underlying tissues. The holes were then joined by cutting the intervening bone with a thing called a Gigli saw, which resembles a particularly vicious garotte made of wire with cutting edges (think of tiny scale barbed wire). This is moved backwards and forwards from underneath the skull outwards, cutting through the bone very effectively. Once the cuts are complete, the piece of skull can be removed to allow access to the blood clot.

After several years of using this system, we had a visit from a senior neurosurgical trainee from Australia called Holly, and she very kindly organised for us to receive a donation of an ex-demonstration, high-speed electric craniotome from a company in Australia which was incomparably better and faster.

Many patients are extremely grateful for the treatment they receive, and over the years, I have received many gifts of different types. These included 6 bottles of an incredibly fine red wine (Chateau Mouton Rothschild for those in the know), a coffee and walnut cake, 50 kg bags of rice, bunches of coconuts, mangoes, bananas, oranges and other assorted fruits, chickens (both dead and alive!), eggs (not sure which came first), a bucket of eels and my particular favourite—a box of live frogs!

My brother commented that the latter was entirely appropriate for me quoting the expression, "Mad as a box of frogs." Needless to say, the more unusual gifts were from the people in Cambodia. I have always found it humbling to see people who have so little wanting to make a gift which is often one they can ill-afford.

In Cambodia, as for the rest of the world, 2020 was the start of a difficult period because of the Covid-19 pandemic. In fact, we were not as badly affected as some countries, although accurate statistics are hard to come by. Nevertheless, the government instituted a strong vaccination programme early on, initially using the Chinese vaccines and later on supplementing these with the more effective mRNA vaccines. This was assisted by the donation of large numbers of vaccines from various countries, including the UK.

Although many cases and deaths went unreported, the overall impression was that the extent of the disease was less widespread than in many countries. Early in in the pandemic, however, there was the same uncertainty as to how best to manage outbreaks in terms of quarantine and so on. In Battambang, the government referral hospital was designated as the primary health facility for severe cases, and our hospital was asked to operate as an overflow facility if the referral hospital became overloaded. Isolation facilities were constructed using acres of plastic sheeting and wooden frames around the beds in one of the wards. In fact, we never needed to use this as we did not receive a single patient. All positively identified cases were sent initially to the referral hospital and, if the patients were well enough, they were quarantined at home until they had consecutive negative tests.

Early on in the pandemic, we had a patient who was incidentally found to be positive on routine testing, and subsequently, a nurse who had been in contact with her also tested positive. The public health department's response to this was to immediately quarantine the entire hospital along with the 70-or-so staff who were working in it at the time (me included). This meant that we were all stranded in the hospital for 2 weeks!

A system was set up so that relatives could deliver a change of clothes and other essential items with a system reminiscent of a prison (without the bag checks or visiting rights). The relative could only approach to within 1 metre of the locked gates (remember social distancing?) and leave the bag on the ground, after which, one of the security guards would pass it through to the recipient behind the locked hospital gates.

Food deliveries were also allowed, and the hospital kitchen did a great job of feeding us all (the kitchen staff were in the same situation as the rest of us) and we had a rota to help them to prepare vegetables and so on for the meals. Sleeping arrangements were impromptu—we were not allowed to use the hospital beds, of course, so many of us slept on the floor of our office or in some of the other administrative offices. Once word got out of our predicament, however, many organisations sought to help out, and we received many generous food donations from other clinics, past patients and one local church which cooked evening meals, placed them into takeaway containers, and delivered them each day!

We were really touched by the display of love and kindness. Although I did, at the time, possess the board game entitled 'Pandemic' at home, I did not feel that this would be well-received as a pastime at the hospital, but we were fairly inventive as far as finding ways to pass the time. One of the people who was 'trapped' with us was Titus, a high-school student from the USA who was on a placement at the hospital for work experience. His parents were living and working in Battambang at the time. He thought the whole thing was brilliant and thoroughly enjoyed himself. He has now gone on to become an advanced emergency medical technician back in the States.

I used a system of lines on the wall to count off the 15 days—I would have been OK in prison, I reckon! Fortunately, the hospital is blessed with a small but beautiful garden, so we were able to get some fresh air. I also spent time running round and round the hospital grounds for exercise, although after the first thirty laps or so, it began to get rather repetitive, and the distance covered was small!

From my own point of view, however, this was a considerable improvement on one of my other periods of quarantine (I spent a lot of time in quarantine for various reasons), where my wife and I were confined to a single room in a hotel in Phnom Penh which we were not allowed to leave for 2 weeks. Meals were delivered and left outside the door. The window was also locked, but having plenty of time on my hands, I managed to pick that, so at least we could get some outside air. We also had an interesting view over the Mekong River. I think it says a lot for our marriage that we both survived intact (or perhaps, my wife's incredible patience with me)!

We both read a lot of books, and I had some lectures to prepare for, which took a good deal of time (probably my best lectures ever). Our day also revolved around highlights such as the mid-morning cup of coffee and the door knock accompanied by the sound of rapidly retreating footsteps indicating the delivery of the next meal. The system the government was using at the time for people returning to Cambodia was to bus them from the airport using what was nicknamed the mystery bus as no one knew where it was going to end up. There was a variety of hotels in Phnom Penh being used—some good, some awful, and it was potluck as to which one the bus would go to, so we were very grateful to discover that we were at one of the good ones where at least the food was edible and the room comfortable.

One of the cultural adjustments that I needed to make in practising medicine in Cambodia was language-related. There are certain, what I hesitate to call idiosyncrasies, partly because I find it difficult to spell, but more particularly because it is just different from what I was used to. One or two examples will allow you to make up your own minds.

The first was the surprising revelation from a patient with a persistent cough who said they were coughing up blue sputum. I had never encountered this before, so seeking clarification from my interpreter, I was told that many people in Cambodia use the same word for both blue and green! I have tried, unsuccessfully, to find out why this might be, but it is certainly widespread.

Another example relates to the person describing their symptoms in terms of their organs, so a typical complaint will be, "Doctor, I have pain in my fallopian tubes." Sometimes, this designation is correct, but I have learnt to always ask the patient to show me where that is, and quite frequently, the pain is in a totally different location to the organ mentioned because anatomical knowledge is not very prevalent. The literal translation of certain diseases from Khmer to English can produce some interesting terms, so haemorrhoids are called coconut roots and epilepsy is mad pig disease (but then I suppose we have mad cow disease in the UK.)

There are also some symptoms described that I still find difficult to explain even after many years as I have never encountered them outside of Cambodia. For example, people will say that they do not have a fever, but they feel hot all over their body. I did wonder whether this equated to menopausal flushing, but men also describe the same symptoms. The vast majority of the population of Cambodia speak Khmer, but there are some regional variations in both pronunciation as well as words and, on occasions, my Khmer colleagues have been as baffled by a word as me.

My clumsy attempts at speaking Khmer have also produced some amusing incidents. I am spoilt, as the hospital where I work uses English as its official language among staff. However, I try and use Khmer on occasions, and one day, in the operating theatre, I accidentally asked for a fish rather than a pair of scissors whilst operating—the two words in Khmer being somewhat similar! My son, who was an exceptional speaker of Khmer, used to tell of mispronouncing a word. He thought meant God's kingdom turning it into God's diarrhoea!

Speaking of coconut roots, we were just finishing a clinic in a village one day when we saw a man lying in a hammock—nothing unusual about that in Cambodia where sleeping is an art form, but the gentleman in question was not asleep and was in considerable pain. In fact, he had barely moved out of the hammock for three days because of severe haemorrhoids. He obligingly pulled his trousers down to reveal what my non-medical Khmer colleague described as being like a pair of lips (I cannot use his precise description as it would be considered racist). Certainly, they were some of the largest prolapsed haemorrhoids I had seen, so we took him off to the hospital and removed them for him, for which he was most grateful.

Gunshot wounds are relatively uncommon in Cambodia as very few people possess guns in Cambodia—it is mostly the police and military personnel—but the most recent example I saw was a police officer who was apparently cleaning his handgun when he dropped it, resulting in it firing and shooting him in the

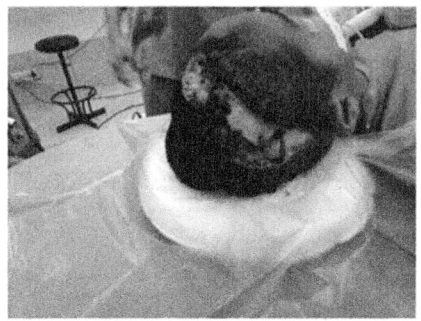

Machete·wound·to·head

chest. I'm not sure whether this is plausible or not, but this was the only history we could elicit, and his colleagues did not seem to be looking for anyone else in connection with the event.

He was fortunate in that the bullet had entered his right lung without causing it to collapse, and it had missed everything important in the area. However, it was quite deeply embedded in his lung, and I felt that on balance, it was safer to leave it alone than to try and remove it, especially as his condition had stabilised after a blood transfusion.

His family disagreed, however, and wanted to have it removed, so they took him off to Thailand, and we have heard nothing further since, so I do not know whether this happened or not. It seems to be a Khmer thing that patients do not like leaving metalwork inside their bodies (I have heard various explanations as to why this might be including the fear that they will get struck by lightning). This particularly relates to plates and rods inserted to stabilise fractures as patients very frequently return asking to have them removed once the fracture has healed.

Apart from gunshots, the other injuries we occasionally see are from machetes or other sharp-bladed weapons. These must be particularly sharp as I have seen several severe injuries including an injury to the hand which cut through the middle of his palm from the little finger to the base of his thumb— the patient having raised his hand to ward off an attack. However, I never discovered what happened to him in the long term as we referred him for specialist treatment and unfortunately no one in Cambodia communicates any follow-up information. Another one produced a deep scalp laceration with the skull cut underneath resulting in a blood clot on the brain.

The most extraordinary, however, was a man who was riding a moto when someone wielding some sort of sword took a swipe at his leg and amputated his foot with a cut through the bone so clean that it looked as if it had been performed surgically. We never really got to the bottom of whether the attack was pre-planned, gang-related or whatever, although we suspect it must have been. Sadly, converting the wound into a functional stump was all that we could do for him.

The climate in Cambodia is a tropical, monsoon one, the country being located just 10 degrees or so north of the equator. The rainy season which typically extends from late May to early November can produce some spectacular downpours and, so far, the extensive drainage works being undertaken around Battambang (and other cities) have failed to relieve flash flooding. Part of the problem is due to large amounts of dropped litter which blocks the drains and part is due to the increasing building, which is typically done on raised up land which increases run off onto the surrounding areas.

Last year was particularly bad, and the emergency room and operating theatre at the hospital were inundated. Even though the flooding may only last for an hour or so, it still leaves the mud behind, which takes considerable work to clean away. Closer to home, our garage was also flooded (we live near a large market which is built on the site of an old lake which was drained before building it) which unfortunately led to the destruction of many of the 10,000 patient record cards I had accumulated over our years of community work.

When I first started work in the village settings, I needed an easy system for recording patient details, diagnoses, prescriptions and so on and, little suspecting how extensive the system would become, I decided to use a card-based system (similar to what many GPs in the UK used before computer records became the norm.) These were filed according to four criteria—village, name, sex and age and stored in plastic boxes for each village. The system has served me well over the years, although it was only after some time that we realised that recording the age was the weak point in the system. We knew from the outset that most people did not know their date of birth, so we merely used stated age, but it became clear that many people did not know their age, either, and so, would just hazard a guess, which often changed from visit to visit.

We have also observed several situations where parents had trouble remembering the name of their children or spouses as everyone tends to use generic titles related to the relative ages of the people involved, whether family, friends or strangers. After each clinic, I added summary data to my trusty Excel spreadsheet, which is how I know I have seen just over 10,000 new patients (plus a further 20,000 on return visits).

I am an inveterate hoarder, so I had kept all of these, even for those villages we no longer visited, so it forced me to dispose of these and things are now more manageable. Fortunately, a lot of the ones I was still using were not irretrievably damaged. A computer-based system was just not feasible due to lack of reliable internet, electricity and so on in the outlying areas. However, I do use the World Health Organisation's anthropometric data recording system for monitoring children's growth. This has proved to be particularly useful in some school health screening we undertook for an NGO we work alongside as it allowed us to produce summary reports for the whole cohort. This confirmed what we had long suspected, namely that there is still significant stunting of growth due to poor nutrition amongst children in Cambodia.

The weather can result in a variety of hazards. I have already mentioned that Cambodians sometimes fear being struck by lightning if they have metalwork in their bodies, but the risk of this happening anyway is not insignificant. In 2023, 84 people were killed by lightning, with a further 59 injured according to the national committee for disaster management. This is partly due to the frequency of electrical storms and partly because there is so much flat, open space in the countryside which is dominated by rice fields. In fact, one of our Khmer friends was very close to a lightning strike two years ago, although fortunately, he was not injured, and my wife witnessed a lightning strike just outside our house.

I had a lesser experience a few years ago when I was out running in the rain (the best time, as it is cooler), and there was a lightning strike in a field about 200 metres away. Interestingly I felt that a strike was imminent for about 30 seconds before it occurred—something to do with the way the air around me felt different from normal; maybe a buildup of static electricity or something—difficult to explain but it did lessen the fright I got a little when it happened. Certainly, the thunderstorms here can be extremely dramatic with lightning every few seconds, sometimes for an hour or more.

The other hazard is flooding and high-water levels in rivers. This is particularly dangerous because many children in Cambodia do not know how to swim but do love to play in the water. This may be relatively harmless such as the children you sometimes see lying down at the side of flooded roads, waiting for the waves of water from passing traffic to wash over them. The biggest risk here is probably gastroenteritis from swallowing some of the disgusting water!

Unfortunately, however, drowning is a big problem and in 2021 Cambodia was ranked the 12th-most dangerous country for deaths by drowning with over 1100 cases, most of which occurred in children and young adults. We encountered one such case in a village where we were holding a clinic. We were approached by the family of a teenager who had gone into an irrigation ditch near a sluice gate to the river to rescue his younger brother but had himself become trapped.

Unfortunately, by the time we got to the site, although he had been pulled out of the water, he was dead, and our resuscitation attempts were unsuccessful. His death, although tragic, did result in him having saved the life of his brother.

The main hospital corridor at the Handa Medical Centre is decorated with a variety of interesting photographs of patients, staff and visitors. One of these shows a well-known actress and her husband at the time on one of their visits to Battambang. She has strong links to the area through her adopted son as well as her filming Tomb Raider, and she has also set up an organisation the Maddox Jolie Pitt foundation, which acts to help relieve extreme poverty in the area. She has a house in the countryside not so far from Battambang. I have never met her despite her having visited on several occasions and having a good rapport with the hospital and our medical director, Dr Gerlinda Lucas.

During the filming of 'First They Killed My Father', the hospital acted as standby for any medical emergencies or accidents, but I was away at the time, and I missed her on a visit prior to that as well. My former colleague, a rather flamboyant Swiss surgeon, was more fortunate and was invited to lunch following his helping the family with a medical emergency. In fact, he was sent a helicopter in order to transport him from Battambang to Siem Reap!

The other famous person featured in one of the pictures is Jackie Chan, but his visit predated my time at the hospital. A less well-known but eminent Belgian doctor who visited was one of the pioneers in discovering the deadly Ebola virus, which has caused many outbreaks in Africa over the past 45 years. I did have the pleasure of meeting him, and he was a very approachable and humble man. I have also had the privilege of meeting Dan Carter, who will be known to any rugby fans as probably the best fly-half ever to play for the All-Blacks (perhaps he should have been called Dan Carlsberg). I will not say best in the world as all the British Lions' fans would cry foul for overlooking his contemporary from the British Lions who, Dan himself told me, he thought was the best, but I think that was just a show of his modesty. He visited the hospital last year and made a big impression on a large group of school children he introduced to rugby (part of another project supported by the Handa Foundation in Battambang) and the nurses who mobbed this tall, handsome athletic foreigner for selfies!

Dan Carter and nurses at Handa Medical Centre

Chapter 7
Never Say Never

I remember being told that you should never say never in medicine, and it is a good piece of advice as one can always get caught out by the exception to the rule. People are not machines, and sometimes, the normal rules just do not seem to apply, and this makes things somewhat unpredictable, but also interesting and challenging.

Another maxim I was taught sounds very confusing (especially when trying to explain it to someone for whom English is a second language) but I have found it helpful is "An uncommon presentation of a common condition is more common than a common presentation of an uncommon one!" The point is that when faced with a patient in whom the diagnosis is not immediately clear, one should think of common conditions which might be presenting in an unusual manner before resorting to more exotic diagnoses.

A recent example of this was a 15-year-old girl who had developed diarrhoea and increasing abdominal swelling and had been admitted to the government hospital with suspected intestinal obstruction (blockage) or gastroenteritis. After 10 days of treatment, she was no better, however, and her parents brought her to our emergency department. She was certainly very distended and tender throughout her abdomen. She did not have a fever, but there were other signs of infection, and we decided to perform an exploratory operation which revealed an advanced case of peritonitis due to perforation of her appendix. If she had been older or less fit, she could easily have died from this.

Despite the never-say-never maxim, I was taught that haemorrhoids (piles) do not bleed enough to cause anaemia, so one should always check for other diagnoses before blaming the haemorrhoids; so when a gentleman came to us complaining of bleeding from his haemorrhoids and a dangerously low blood count (haemoglobin) of 3.7 g/dl (normal above 13 g/dl), I was pretty convinced there was something else going on. Nevertheless, after a careful search of his digestive tract, we found no other cause and, after removing his haemorrhoids, his blood count returned to normal. This was only the second case of haemorrhoid-induced anaemia I had seen in 30 years of surgical practice.

I rarely saw patients with such low blood counts before coming to Cambodia where such values are commonplace, but I recall one man in his thirties in Bishop Auckland who came to see me in my clinic. I recognised him as he was quite short, very thin and extremely athletic. I had seen him on several occasions out running around the town, and he never looked well, but I put this down to his exertion. Funnily enough, his complaint was that he was finding it more and more difficult to run as he was getting out of breath, and he was also feeling tired all the time.

He certainly looked even more unwell than usual, and further investigation revealed his blood count to be 4.5 g/dl, so I was surprised he could even walk, let alone run. It turned out he had a large, benign polyp in his upper intestine, which had been bleeding slowly over a long period of time, producing his anaemia. Once we had removed this, which we managed to do through a camera inserted via his mouth, he made a rapid recovery and returned to just looking unwell when he was running. Nevertheless, his running speed improved dramatically!

The other reason I used the chapter title is because of the existence of so-called never events. This is a concept in medicine which classifies certain serious complications of medical treatment (known as iatrogenic problems) as being so severe that they should never occur. Examples of this would include things such as giving a patient the wrong blood for transfusion, operating on the wrong limb and so on. Unfortunately, they still do occur, and this is a global health issue—most of the time, these errors occur as a result of system failures rather than being a mistake made by one individual, and often, there will be a sequence of events that result in the unwanted outcome.

As healthcare professionals will tell you, no one goes to work intending to harm patients (with a couple of notable exceptions from recent years). All doctors know the so-called Hippocratic injunction 'Primum non nocere', which, translated from Latin, means "First, do no harm." In fact, this does not appear to have originated from Hippocrates but seems to have appeared in the medical literature in the 1860s and is thought to be attributable to Thomas Syndenham, an English physician who lived in the 17th century and who described a neurological condition which now bears his name—Sydenham's chorea.

We recently witnessed the result of one such event when a young woman in her early thirties came to our surgical clinic because of a severe wound infection. She had undergone an operation to remove her appendix at another hospital some two weeks earlier and initially made a good recovery, but then her wound started to discharge a lot of pus. She went back to the hospital where the surgeon decided to explore her wound to help to control the infection, and during the operation, he discovered a surgical swab which had been left inside. Fortunately, once this had been removed, her wound started to heal, and after a few more weeks, it had completely closed, and although she has a rather ugly scar, she has no other adverse effects.

Another serious complication I saw a number of years ago was a man who had been admitted to another hospital in Cambodia following a road traffic accident. He had bleeding in his chest on the right side—a haemothorax, and the doctor attempted to insert a chest drain to remove the blood. This is a plastic tube approximately one centimetre in diameter. This failed to drain anything except for a small amount of fresh blood and some yellowish fluid. He was sent to our hospital with the chest drain still in place, and it was apparent that it had been inserted too low down on the chest and the tip had, in fact, entered his liver (hence the yellowish fluid which was bile) which is below the diaphragm rather than going into the chest cavity above the diaphragm.

Surprisingly, his condition was stable, and we removed the tube, kept him on bedrest under careful observation for 48 hours and then started to get him up, following which he had no problems and so we were able to discharge him without the need for any surgery. Fortunately, the problem had been on his right side, because if the same had occurred on the left, the drain would have hit his spleen where the risk of serious bleeding would have been much higher.

These cases pale into insignificance, however, when compared to the man I saw one day at the hospital here in Cambodia. He had some abdominal symptoms and, when I examined him, I saw he had two old surgical scars in his lower abdomen—one on each side. I confirmed with him that the one on his right was from having his appendix removed, but when I asked him what the one on the left side was, he explained that the surgeon had initially operated on that side looking for his appendix on the wrong side! This had happened many years earlier, but I do not think that human anatomy has changed much in the intervening period, and the patient was not suffering from the incredibly rare condition of situs inversus where all the internal organs are transposed from their normal positions.

I did see a patient with the less rare condition called dextrocardia when the heart is on the opposite side of the chest from normal (i.e. right, not left). The patient had been seen following a moto accident with a fractured clavicle, and so, had a chest X-ray taken. We initially thought that the radiographer had perhaps mislabelled the left and right side on the X-ray (so-called technical dextrocardia), but on closer inspection, the patient's stomach could be seen on the left side under the diaphragm as usual, so the diagnosis was confirmed.

The patient had no symptoms attributable to this but was surprised by the subsequent queue of nurses and doctors wanting to listen to his chest! This probably ranks number two in my all-time strange clinical findings in the chest. "What was number one?" I hear you cry—well, you probably will cry when I tell you.

Allow me to set the scene: An elderly and very obese, diabetic lady was admitted to the ward (we are back in the UK now), and as the house officer, my job was to perform a thorough check-up of all her body systems. Part of this was to examine her chest and listen to her heart. She had very large and pendulous breasts, and I needed to lift her left breast skywards to be able to place my stethoscope in the appropriate position on her chest wall.

As I lifted her breast, I was greeted with an appalling odour (not one in my repertoire of recognisable smells), but I initially attributed this to what we call intertrigo, which is a fungal infection that sometimes occurs between skin folds. However, I then noticed a large mass of creamy coloured material in the fold between her breast and her chest wall. It was at this stage that I wished I had put gloves on prior to examining her. Fishing this out, I became increasingly disturbed by what it might be—some sort of tumour perhaps?

As I held it aloft, she declared, "Oh, so that is where it went!"

"What do you mean?" I asked.

"Well, I was eating a cheese sandwich in bed about a week ago, and I dropped it and could not find it in the bed."

You know how cheddar cheese is sold in packs with a grade for flavour/maturity of the cheese. This would have been well off the scale! I couldn't face eating cheese sandwiches for some time after that. It reminds me of a joke about sandwiches. Three men worked on a high-rise building at a construction site—

an Englishman, a Scot and an Irishman. They used to sit on top of the building for their lunchbreak, and all had a packed lunch of sandwiches.

One day, the Englishman opened his lunch box and said, "Oh no. Jam sandwiches again. I am sick and tired of jam sandwiches. If I get them again tomorrow, I am going to jump off the building!" The Scot opened his lunch and declared, "Oh no. Peanut butter sandwiches again. I am sick and tired of peanut butter sandwiches. If I get them again tomorrow, I will join you!" The Irishman opened his lunch and said, "Oh, no. Cheese sandwiches again. If I get them again tomorrow, I will join both of you."

Anyway, the following day, the Englishman had jam sandwiches again, so he jumped, followed by the Scot who had peanut butter again, and then the Irishman who had cheese once more. At the funeral, the widows were all commiserating with each other.

The wife of the Englishman said, "I can't understand it. I thought he loved jam sandwiches."

The Scotsman's wife said, "I can't believe it either. I thought he really liked peanut butter sandwiches."

The Irishman's wife then said, "I can't believe it. He used to make his own sandwiches!"

Foreign materials inserted into the human body either unintentionally or deliberately have always been a cause for concern, and there have been numerous cases of problems resulting from them. In the UK, amongst other countries, there have been the recent high-profile cases of serious complications after the insertion of transvaginal mesh for treatment of urinary incontinence and prolapse, resulting in the Independent Medicines and Medical Devices Safety review, and the subsequent report was entitled "First do no harm!"

Of course, there are many examples of foreign materials being used with great success—one only has to think of fracture management with metalwork of various kinds as well as joint replacements, prosthetic heart valves and hernia repair meshes. The biggest risk with all of these implants is infection which can occur early, usually due to a failure of surgical or operating room technique or late which by definition occurs more than one year following surgery and is mostly due to bacteria in the bloodstream (bacteraemia) settling on the implant. This is a small but ever-present risk and cannot be prevented.

An example I saw was a patient of mine who had undergone repair of a hernia in his groin two and a half years earlier using a standard, open-repair technique with a mesh. He had experienced no problems following the surgery but suddenly developed a painful swelling underneath his scar, and when I saw him, my first thought was that his hernia had recurred. However, when we explored his wound, we discovered the mesh floating in a pool of pus. We never discovered the source of the bacteria, but the sudden onset of the infection so long after surgery strongly suggested it was indeed bloodborne.

When I was a surgical trainee in Newcastle in the 1980s, we had a most unusual and unfortunate case of bacteraemia-related complications. It was a young man about 20 years old who had developed an ingrowing toenail which he tried to cut but which then got infected with staphylococcus (not MRSA), a common bacterium often found on the skin. He developed bacteraemia at some point, which probably would not have been a big problem, were it not for the fact that it was subsequently discovered that he had been born with an abnormal heart valve, and the bacteria settled on this and started to grow.

This condition, known as infective endocarditis, is a serious disease, and it caused his aortic valve to stop working properly, and he needed to undergo an emergency open-heart procedure to replace it. As if this was not bad enough, he then proceeded to develop a series of what are known as septic emboli, which are blood clots containing bacteria which travel through the bloodstream and get lodged in various places around the body. The most serious of these was in the artery leading to his spleen.

This produced a widening of the artery (aneurysm), which burst, leading to sudden and life-threatening haemorrhage, and he needed emergency surgery to control the bleeding and resulted in him having his spleen removed. He also developed one in his leg (the one with the ingrowing toenail) which blocked a small artery leading to gangrene of his big toe which had to be amputated (ironically thereby preventing any further ingrowing toenail problems). In total he was in hospital for almost six months, and all because of an ingrowing toenail.

In the UK and many other countries, there is extensive regulation of medical implants which have to go through an exhaustive approval process before they can be used. Unfortunately, this does not always prevent problems which may occur long after the implant has been inserted. Examples of this include some of the early breast implants using silicone (of which I have no experience) and a device used for a time in the 1980s to treat oesophageal reflux which causes heartburn.

The device in question appeared to be both simple to use and effective. It was a thing that looked rather like a ring doughnut and was placed surgically around the lower end of the oesophagus where it joins the stomach and then secured with a tape. Unfortunately, a number of reports began to emerge of serious complications where it either migrated somewhere else or ulcerated through the oesophagus or stomach necessitating its removal.

I saw one patient who had undergone the surgery some years earlier who had initially had successful control of his symptoms, but then went on to develop difficulty swallowing. When we performed a camera examination of his stomach, we discovered that half of the prosthesis had penetrated the wall of his stomach and was causing an obstruction. I have also seen a case where a patient had insertion of a laparoscopic band around the upper stomach for treatment of morbid obesity and developed the same symptoms, but on this occasion, in addition to the band perforating the stomach, it appeared to have been inserted through a loop of small intestine as we discovered when we performed the surgery to remove it. Remarkably, he had not come to any harm from this latter mishap.

Other things can also migrate within the body with rare cases of bullets passing into and along blood vessels and even rarer cases of patients coughing up bullets many years after having been shot in the lung! A rather more rapid migration I saw was a case of a patient who had undergone fixation of a fracture of the upper part of the humerus (upper arm) using Kirschener wires (or K-wires as they are commonly referred to). These are basically lengths of straight, stiff metal, a couple of millimetres in diameter, which hold the two ends of the bone in place whilst healing occurs. They are cut to length and usually bent over at the end. They are often left protruding through the skin to allow for easy removal after a few weeks.

On this occasion, the ends had not been bent over, and the patient was admitted a few weeks after surgery with a sudden onset of chest pain and shortness of breath. An X-ray of the chest revealed that one of the K-wires had migrated from the fracture, underneath the skin and had then punctured the patient's lung. It was subsequently retrieved, and a chest tube inserted to allow the collapsed lung to re-inflate.

My experience with implants in Cambodia has been limited to the use of mesh in hernia repairs. Because of financial constraints (surgical meshes are very expensive) and supply difficulties, we started to use an easily sourced local material in the form of sterilised mosquito netting. This is freely available, very cheap and forms a brilliant alternative to the so-called lightweight synthetic meshes used elsewhere.

I hasten to add that we were not the pioneers of this technique as it had been reported in the surgical literature from India with good results. We have now been using this for over 10 years in more than 100 patients, and there have been no significant adverse effects. In fact, I think it is at least as good as the 'official' meshes with which I had extensive experience in the UK. Here, at least is one example of less regulation being a benefit rather than a hazard.

Chapter 8
No Sex Please, We're British

I took this title from a British farce performed in the West End in the early 1970s, which was then made into a film featuring Ronnie Corbett, Arthur Lowe and Beryl Reid, and it became a popular catchphrase thereafter.

An interesting contrast between British and Cambodian cultures is the attitude towards contraception methods, and in particular, vasectomy. In the UK, vasectomy is a long-standing and widely accepted method of contraception, but in Cambodia, it is largely shunned. Part of the reason for this, one of my Khmer medical friends explains, is that the word used to describe it in Khmer implies castration!

Anyway, the only men upon whom I have performed vasectomies in Cambodia have been either expats or Khmer who have worked with and known expats for many years and who have undergone a vasectomy and come safely through, bits intact. Not everyone in the UK is convinced of the benefits, however, and I think that sometimes pressure is applied by the spouse.

I remember a patient who, having been through the whole explanation, consent and pre-operative preparation for the procedure, got cold feet (or should that be cold something else?) at the last minute and absconded from the waiting room minutes before he was due to undergo the procedure, never to be seen again! At the other extreme was a man who, during the procedure, asked me how long he would have to wait before having sex after the operation. Quick as a flash, the (female) nurse who was assisting me said, "Well, I think you had better wait until you get home first!"

I worked for a time with an American doctor who had worked in Cambodia for many years who told me, in a very matter-of-fact way, that he had performed his own vasectomy many years earlier! I was so taken aback that I didn't ask him for details of how he managed this—did he use mirrors, was he sitting down, etc.? This is certainly not something I would recommend, but he said that he could not find anyone to do it at the time as no one in Cambodia had any experience with vasectomies. I still think that the use of alternative methods of contraception might have been both safer and preferable.

In order to be fully effective, vasectomies are performed in various ways to prevent the two ends of the divided tube (the vas deferens—hence, VASectomy) from joining back together. We still cite the possibility of this occurring at about 1 in 2000 cases—I have never seen it, but then, I haven't performed 2000 vasectomies! A far more likely cause for a pregnancy occurring after a successful vasectomy is the involvement of a third party (traditionally rendered as the milkman). Sometimes, circumstances change after someone has had a vasectomy, and the man will come requesting a reversal of the procedure.

Surgeons have had varying attitudes towards performing this procedure, which is technically trickier, but the most extreme was a urologist I knew who didn't believe in it at all and counselled his patients to that effect before performing the operation. He also removed about four times the length of each vas than was standard, saying, "I'd like to see someone reverse that!"

Men are always being told, or possibly telling themselves, that size does not matter. Clearly, some men do not believe this, and I saw a young Cambodian man a couple of years ago who had taken matters into his own hands, so to speak. He came to me complaining of pain in his penis, but no urinary symptoms or anything suggestive of a sexually transmitted disease. When I examined him, his penis looked swollen, red and scarred. On further questioning, he admitted to injecting oil under the skin to make himself bigger. The problem was the type of oil he had used (some sort of cosmetic application, I think), which had produced a severe irritation resulting in inflammation and scarring. In fact, it was so bad that we had to excise some of the worst-affected areas.

It appears that this is not such an uncommon practice, and I have seen a further case, although fortunately, the reaction was less severe and eventually settled with some medication. Although I have no experience with the procedure, I am aware that injection of the patient's own fat cells has been used in a similar manner, so in a way, the principle is established, but of course, there is no risk of reaction to your own fat.

A more serious condition is cancer of the penis, and sadly, as with so many other diseases, it often presents late. Perhaps, this is due to embarrassment as sometimes, men initially think they may have a sexually transmitted disease, but also, it is a surprisingly painless condition. However, the most advanced case I recall was of a man who saw one of my past bosses and who stated that his penis had dropped off whilst he was passing urine. He had rescued it from the toilet bowl and brought it with him. Examination of the patient revealed extensive ulceration and erosion near the base of his penis which had led to the separation.

A common source of penile injuries is due to the foreskin becoming trapped in a trouser zipper (usually jeans, for some reason). Although I always assumed this was only a problem in men who did not wear underpants, apparently the use of underwear does not offer complete protection. The solution to the problem is to cut the zipper free from the trousers and then separate the two halves from the closed end. The injury itself, although painful, is rarely serious enough to need any other intervention apart from routine wound care. What is amusing to see is the expression on the face of the patient when they first see the large pair of scissors being wielded by the person who is going to cut the zipper out, thinking they are about to have a circumcision!

A much less common situation I encountered was a man who had devised a new take on 'the ship in a bottle' ornament that you see from time to time proudly displayed on mantelpieces and display cabinets in people's homes. This one was unsuitable for displaying anywhere as he had substituted his penis for the ship. I cannot remember what type of bottle it was, except that it was unfortunately made of glass.

When he arrived, the constriction of the neck of the bottle had resulted in extensive swelling, preventing removal of the bottle, and attempts to apply lubricants were unsuccessful. Another technique would have been to try and aspirate blood from his penis as one does for priapism, but the glass bottle, of course, precluded this. Further brainstorming produced only one possible solution in the form of a hammer! We had to go to the maintenance department to select a suitable one. (What is a suitable hammer for this job?) This time, the look of apprehension on his face was entirely appropriate, but amazingly, we were able to break the bottle without inducing any serious injury to the patient. I do not feel this was our finest hour in terms of sophisticated medical treatment, but the patient was nevertheless very relieved.

It is a surprising fact that two of the best healing areas of skin on the body are the region immediately around the anus and the scrotum. For example, a patient who has had haemorrhoids surgically removed will initially have two or three open wounds around their anus. (3,7 and 11 o'clock, remember?) On review six weeks later, it is sometimes almost impossible to see the scars. Equally fascinating, at least to me, is that the wounds virtually never (note: I do not say never!) get infected.

In fact, I can only recall one case of a postoperative infection after haemorrhoid surgery, and this occurred in the UK whilst I was working for a very methodical colorectal specialist, who had performed a completely routine haemorrhoidectomy and was shocked to see the patient return to the emergency department a week later with a horrible infection that eventually required a temporary colostomy to control. We looked for all sorts of possible underlying causes such as diabetes and various bowel disorders but found none—so we never really got to the bottom of it, so to speak.

As far as the scrotum is concerned, I recall an unfortunate man who developed a fearsome complication of his diabetes in the form of necrotising fasciitis (think 'flesh-eating bacteria' of the tabloid press). This was affecting his groin area and upper thigh as well as extending to his scrotum. The only way to control this, in addition to antibiotics, is radical surgery to remove all the affected skin and, in his case, it left him with his testicles literally dangling in the breeze, looking like the clackers toy that was popular in the 1970s and which, for some reason, enjoyed a renaissance in Cambodia a couple of years ago. These comprise a pair of plastic balls, each attached by a string to a handle. We needed to apply skin grafts to his thigh, but his scrotal skin healed so rapidly without intervention that after a few weeks it looked completely normal.

When I was a final-year medical student, I spent a few weeks on a psychiatric ward (not as a patient, I hasten to add). I really enjoyed psychiatry, and, for a while, this was jostling for top position in my career choice with surgery being the other—well, you can see which one won, but there is quite a lot of overlap. I remember a plastic surgeon telling me that if you want to see psychiatric patients, go to a plastic surgery outpatient clinic.

One of the patients I saw gave a bit of an insight into this as she was suffering from a condition called dysmorphophobia. In essence, this causes patients to have delusional beliefs about their own body. This lady in particular had two—first of all, she felt that her facial profile when seen from one side was perfectly normal, but when seen from the other side was abnormal. She spent considerable time trying to convince me of this by turning her head in different directions and asking me if I could see her deformity.

Her second delusion related to one of her big toes which she felt was abnormal, and she was very self-conscious about it. She also informed me that when she watched the news on television, the newsreader kept looking down at her toe (when he was, of course, reading his notes). Sometimes, the delusions are much more subtle, and it is these people who may seek help from plastic surgeons to correct their perceived deformities, and so, a basic psychological assessment can be an important step prior to undertaking cosmetic surgical procedures. Naturally, the majority of people do not fall into this category, but this was the point the plastic surgeon was making.

One component of a psychiatric assessment is to take a sexual history from the patient, and I was asked to interview a lady with bipolar disorder and then present the history back to my supervising consultant. As I finished my case presentation, he asked me, "What about her sexual history?" To that, I replied without thinking, "Oh, it is up and down," which caused him a great deal of amusement at my expense.

At least my encounter was better than that of a good friend with whom I shared lodgings. When he did his psychiatric attachment, he was asked to talk to a different lady with bipolar disorder who was currently in a manic stage. Apparently, she declared her undying love for him and spent most of the interview asking him to marry her—she even had a ring!

Part of my reason for the choice of title for this chapter was the stereotypical British prudence regarding many bodily processes. However, as recent TV series such as 'Embarrassing Bodies' have shown, there are a substantial minority of people who have more exhibitionist tendencies. I mean, would you really want pictures of your butt being screened throughout the country?

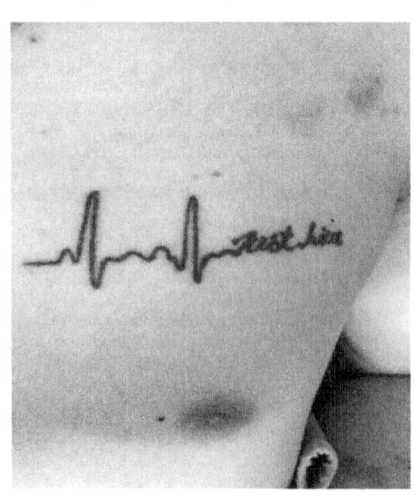

Realistic ECG Tattoo

I suppose the darker recesses of social media have also allowed this sort of behaviour to thrive. I have only had limited encounters of this sort as most of my patients display a degree of modesty that one might expect when discussing intimate matters. There are exceptions to this, of course, and sometimes they occur in the most surprising settings.

Khmer women are generally particularly modest and are very embarrassed if they need to be examined—especially if they need a breast examination. At the hospital in Battambang, I am blessed with a female surgical trainee who will perform the examination of those patients who feel uncomfortable being examined by a man. Interestingly, however, they often prefer me, as a foreigner, to one of my male Khmer colleagues. Perhaps, it is because I am older.

Anyway, I was performing a clinic in one of the villages recently. These tend to be rather public affairs at the best of times as we hold them outside or under cover of the local pagoda, and all the patients, families and friends tend to gather into one big group, usually surrounding the consulting area. A lady came up and, when asked what her problem was, promptly pulled up her top to reveal her chest for all to see in order to show me her breast lump!

I was somewhat nonplussed, but she didn't seem bothered in the slightest. We did move her to a slightly more private location when the time came to examine her. Examining patients sometimes leads to amusing discoveries. I once met a little old lady in her 80s who was wearing knickers emblazoned with the word 'TIGER' on them. Then there was the young woman with green pubic hair and a tattoo saying, "Keep off the grass," and various tattoos saying things like "Cut here" above a dotted line, although I have yet to see one in the correct position for a proposed surgical procedure.

I also had a nurse with whom I worked, who came to see me as a patient, and she needed a rectal examination, during the course of which I noticed a small butterfly tattoo on her bottom. For some reason, she was more embarrassed about this than the rectal examination. I have also seen a number of 'ECG' tattoos. These purport to show an electrocardiograph tracing, and some are more accurate than others. In fact, the most realistic one I have seen was here in Cambodia.

If you want to see some of the more offbeat (forgive the pun) ones, an internet search for ECG tattoos will show you the variety. There is even a doctor on TikTok who has been rating them. I have noticed, however, that the availability of smartphones and their associated cameras has led to an increasing number of patients showing me pictures of their haemorrhoids, intestinal worms, faeces and so on. In some cases, this can be quite helpful, although sometimes, I wonder what would happen if they lost their phone… I also get images sent on messenger and by email—there is nothing I enjoy more than opening a message from someone whilst eating breakfast to be confronted with images of their last bowel motion or sputum sample!

The absence of a camera does not always deter someone from providing an impromptu update on their medical condition. I was once shopping in the Tesco supermarket on the Isle of Man when a voice shouted across from the other end of the store down the aisle, "Hey doc, how are you? You did a great job on my haemorrhoids!"

I also had the somewhat surreal experience of being on holiday at a small beach resort in the South of France with my family when a stranger came up to me and asked if I remembered him. Well, I didn't, but that didn't deter him. He lifted his T-shirt up to show me his extensive abdominal surgical scar, at which point, I realised that I had operated on him a year or so earlier!

Another occasion when a photograph would have been preferable occurred with a rather eccentric lady upon whom I had performed a colostomy some months earlier. She remained convinced that there was some internal problem and used to bring little bits of her poo wrapped in tissue for me to inspect. On one occasion, she told me that she had passed a bone and, sure enough, within the proffered tissue was a small bone which looked like the vertebra of a small rodent. I never managed to find out whether this was an elaborate deception or whether it was something she had eaten, but, after checking her over, I managed to reassure her that all was well.

In the days before smartphones, there was a senior trainee on a medical ward who always insisted on inspecting the bedpan contents of patients who had passed anything unusual during the night. One of my medical student friends, who was working on the ward at the time, relates a prank that the other members of the team played on him. The ward used disposable bedpans made of a sort of fibreboard material, and they had prepared one before the ward round with chocolate mousse (Angel Delight).

On the round, the house officer stated that a particular patient had passed a lot of melaena during the night (this is a black, sticky stool due to the presence of a lot of partially digested blood). As expected, he asked to see it, and when he was shown the bedpan, he looked at it rather suspiciously. "Are you sure that is melaena?" he asked, at which point, the house officer stuck his finger into the contents, licked it and after a moment's hesitation, said, "Yes, definitely melaena!"

Chapter 9
Random Musings of a Disorderly Mind

I have never been a political animal, and in fact, one reason for my choosing district hospital surgical practice over an academic career was because of the politics involved in many teaching hospitals. I always considered it important to be able to work well with one's colleagues rather than appear to be in competition with them, and I have been very fortunate over the years to work with some wonderful people. However, sometimes, events created unexpected circumstances, and one of those was when I was working in Bishop Auckland General Hospital in 2001.

There were a lot of changes going on in the provision of hospital services in County Durham at the time involving the setting up of NHS trusts and merging some services. One of the results of this was that the Central Sterile Services Department (CSSD) for our hospital was moved to a hospital 15 miles away, Darlington Memorial Hospital. I should perhaps explain that the instruments, surgical drapes and so on that we use during surgical operations are prepacked into sets which are self-contained. These are sterilised in a large machine called an autoclave using steam under pressure.

Once the operation has been completed, the instruments are cleaned and then repacked and sterilised, ready for their next use. As a result of the relocation of the CSSD, all the instruments had to be transported to Darlington Memorial Hospital for this process to be completed.

One day, during the pre-operative checks by the theatre nurse, it was observed that there were some bits of debris inside the sterile packaging, and on further inspection, this was found to have detached from some of the instruments we were planning to use. In the light of this, I cancelled the planned operation as I did not feel the sterility of the instruments could be guaranteed. In addition, this was not an isolated incident, and I believed it was directly related to the fact that during the time it took to transport the instruments back to the CSSD in Darlington any residual blood and tissue fragments on the instruments had dried and was not adequately removed during the subsequent cleaning.

The lady who was due to have the operation (to remove gallstones) had unfortunately had her operation cancelled once already (for different reasons, I think). She went to see her GP, rather upset about the situation as one might expect (I had explained the circumstances to her). Thereafter, her GP rang me to see what was going on. He, unlike me, was a highly political animal, and insisted on contacting the local press who then ran a story 'Blood and Flesh On'. The interest in the story from the press's point of view was heightened by the fact that Darlington Memorial Hospital was in the constituency of an MP, who just happened to be the minister for health at the time!

I hadn't wanted my name to come up in the article, but it did, of course. However, I took comfort from what someone said to me. "It is OK to be in the newspaper, just as long as you aren't on the front page!" The outcome was that the health minister rapidly became involved, and appropriate changes were made, following which the situation did not recur, so perhaps, it is sometimes good to be political!

The art of communication is obviously vital in medicine, and this has been increasingly recognised over time. This is particularly important when it comes to obtaining consent from the patient for a surgical operation so that the patient can make an informed choice. It is also interesting to note that sometimes, despite our best efforts, misunderstandings can occur.

Many years ago, I saw a woman in her early 30s who was pregnant and who had developed a cancer in her rectum. This is fortunately a highly unusual situation, and after considerable discussion with her and her family, she agreed to undergo surgery to remove the tumour during her pregnancy. She was in the middle third of her pregnancy which is actually the safest time to operate from the point of view of the foetus, and I explained that during the operation, we would carefully hold her uterus out of the wound whilst we performed the surgery (the rectum is behind the uterus which, at this stage reached up to her umbilicus).

The surgery was actually quite straightforward as we were able to position her uterus outside the abdomen, leaving plenty of room to perform the surgery. She made a good recovery, and her pregnancy proceeded uneventfully. The first time she came back to the outpatient clinic a couple of weeks later, she asked me the sex of her baby. She had not asked when she had undergone her prenatal screening and was surprised when I told her I didn't know, and on further questioning, she had thought that we had taken the baby out of her uterus and held it during the operation, before putting it back at the end!

The principles of informed consent and patient autonomy are both crucial in medicine in general, but particularly so in surgery, where patients are essentially agreeing to undergo a serious physical assault in the form of a surgical operation. Long gone are the days of 'the doctor knows what is best for you', although sadly, this attitude still persists in Cambodia, and we now adopt a collaborative approach of working alongside patients to ensure that the decisions they make are well informed. That is not to say that this always results in what is in the patient's best interests and one dramatic case stands out in my mind.

A middle-aged gentleman came to see me one day in my surgical outpatient clinic on the Isle of Man. He was suffering from a serious colonic disorder—ulcerative colitis, which was not responding to medical treatment, and he had been referred by my gastroenterologist colleague for assessment regarding surgical treatment. Unfortunately, this would involve removing his whole colon and rectum, although it would cure him.

During the conversation we were having, he came out with the unexpected statement, "I have sacrificed my health on the altar of my wife's ambition." Being somewhat taken aback by this extraordinary comment, I asked him what he meant, and he basically blamed his chronic bowel problems on the fact that his wife, who was a successful businesswoman in the banking sector, had moved from place to place as she obtained increasingly senior positions. He was unable to work because of his medical condition and appeared to resent her success.

I explained that he really needed to consider surgery in order to regain his health, but he flatly refused to consider it. I thought he might change his mind given an opportunity to think it through, so I arranged a follow-up appointment for him. On this occasion, two things were clear; firstly, that he had not changed his mind, and secondly, that he was going to die if he did not have the operation, and I told him this quite bluntly. Unfortunately, this was to no avail despite my being certain that he understood. I therefore referred him back to my medical colleague to try and help him as best he could, but he did indeed die a few weeks later.

Miscommunication is more likely when there is translation from a foreign language involved, and sometimes, patients do not volunteer information that they do not think important. I have noticed this a lot in Cambodia, and I remember one patient a couple of years ago who, when asked about any previous illnesses, denied that they had had any. After some investigation of their symptoms, it became apparent that they were suffering from tuberculosis. When I explained this to the patient, they said, "Oh, yes. I have been on treatment for that for three months."

Although we try to describe complications that can occur as a result of surgery to patients, we are sometimes caught out. The most extreme example I can think of was when I was a final-year medical student doing a locum on a surgical ward. This was one of the Nightingale wards that I mentioned in a previous chapter, and this played a large role in what happened.

A very frail-looking elderly gentleman (in his late 70s or thereabouts) had undergone a hernia repair the previous day and appeared to be making an uneventful recovery, but the attention of the ward staff was alerted to the fact that he had just started yelling and leapt out of bed. On this particular ward, the windows were tall, but the lower end was at about chest height.

No sooner had he got out of bed than he jumped up onto the windowsill in a remarkably agile movement for anyone, let alone an elderly man recovering from a hernia operation. We decided the best approach was to try and 'talk him down' and reason with him, emulating the police negotiators in many Hollywood movies, but as we approached, he became increasingly agitated and immediately kicked one of the windowpanes which smashed.

I should mention that the ward was on the first floor. At this point, he was holding onto the curtain rail that ran round his bed. As one we immediately decided that the softly, softly approach was not going to work, and in order to prevent him from further injuring himself, we rushed him and grabbed him to pull him off the windowsill. Unfortunately, he continued to hold onto the curtain rail, and we all overbalanced, ending up in a heap on the floor with the patient, curtain rail and curtain crashing down with us.

As I mentioned previously, the Nightingale wards consisted of a single, long room with little privacy, and the reaction of the other 20 or so patients as they witnessed this unfolding scene worthy of a slapstick comedy must have been one of horror. The outcome was that he was surprisingly unhurt (he did land on top of a group of bodies after all), and once sedated, he settled down. It transpired that he had developed a urinary infection, causing an acute confusional state with hallucinations. He (fortunately) remembered little about it!

When the film 'Ghostbusters' was subsequently released, I was reminded of this event by the scene in the library when the ghostbusters encounter a 'full torso apparition' reading a book and, as they quietly approach Ray suddenly shouts, "Get her!" and starts to rush towards it at which she transforms into a monstrous, scary apparition.

A Foley catheter is variously described as an instrument of torture or an invaluable medical device for draining the bladder. It can be the source of various problems, especially in confused patients who tend to pull on it as it is a source of discomfort and irritation. It is retained in place by a fluid-filled balloon on the end which prevents it from slipping out. The size of this varies but typically it is about 2 cm in diameter once inflated.

I have seen a male patient somehow manage to pull this out through his urethra, which must have been incredibly painful. Like all mechanical devices, they sometimes malfunction, and occasionally, the small channel that is used to inflate the balloon can become blocked, meaning that the balloon cannot be deflated. We used to solve this by injecting a small quantity of ether into the channel, which rapidly expands into a vapour when warmed by the bladder and ruptures the balloon. This leads to a small but satisfying pop but also makes the patient jump as they feel the mini shockwave.

Hernias are common and, unless there is something unusual, such as the case described above, they do not get much recognition in descriptions of patient encounters. My next story certainly fulfils the 'unusual' criteria and starts with the letter sent to a GP by a colleague of mine who worked at a district general hospital outside Newcastle.

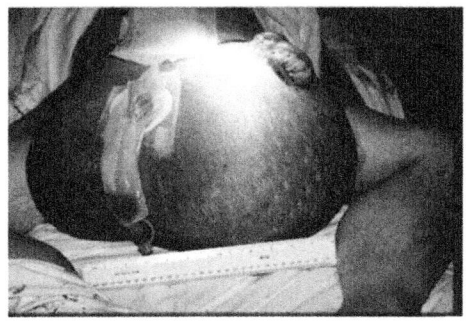

The GP had referred a male patient to him with a right inguinal hernia (the most common hernia occurring in the groin region). The letter started with the line "Dear doctor, thank you for referring this patient with the largest hernia in the history of the universe!" and

Massive Hernia (Note protruding intestine) although that might have been a little overstated, it certainly rated very highly in the list of possible contenders.

He later described the consultation to me, relating how the gentleman had staggered into his clinic wearing a greatcoat which, when removed, revealed a hernia so large it almost touched the floor. A search of the medical literature will provide the definition of a giant inguinoscrotal hernia as one that reaches below the midpoint of the inner thigh when the patient is standing. When a hernia is moderately large, it often extends into the scrotum, and if it is very large, the scrotum becomes hugely enlarged, and there are descriptions of patients with hernias of this size needing a wheelbarrow to support their scrotum.

This of course brings to mind the cartoon character from the British comic Viz called Buster Gonad who was drawn carrying his 'unfeasibly large testicles' in a wheelbarrow. It takes many years for a hernia to develop to this size, but the patient in question would only admit to having had it for a few months, but he did appear to suffer from some psychological problems. My colleague realised that this was beyond a straightforward repair and referred him to one of the surgeons in Newcastle for whom I was currently working.

I was not present at the initial operation which consisted of a combination of an approach via both the scrotum and the abdomen, but unfortunately, this was unsuccessful as attempts to put all the abdominal contents back where they belonged resulted in so much pressure on his diaphragm and other structures that he could not be ventilated, and his blood pressure dropped dangerously. This occurs because, over time, the available space within the abdominal cavity shrinks.

The only solution was to allow the hernia to revert to its original position, but despite this, the lowering of his blood pressure during the operation had damaged his kidneys, and he developed kidney failure, for which he needed a prolonged period of dialysis. Equally unfortunate was the decision by one of the nurses on the renal unit to remove the sutures from the incision on his scrotum before it had completely healed as this resulted in the wound popping open and loops of his intestines spilling out (see photo).

It was at this point that I received an emergency call to go and see him as I was on duty, and we needed to perform further surgery to replace them. This meant merely replacing the intestines within his scrotum as there was still no prospect of being able to repair his hernia. Even this was difficult, but we eventually managed to do so and, in the operation note, I left a clear message that the sutures were not to be removed until assessed by a senior surgeon.

The patient languished on the ward for many months and was unable to get out of bed. His hips were permanently apart in a frog's leg type of position because of the size of the hernia. I subsequently left this surgical unit to move on to my next training job, but I believe that the patient developed further complications and eventually passed away. There are many discussions in the surgical literature about how to manage these, fortunately rare, hernias and mostly focus on ways of increasing the size of the abdominal cavity before attempting to reduce the hernia.

A particular group of patients who always pose a challenge are those who suffer from a greater or lesser degree of hypochondriasis. This can take lots of different forms, but one of the more common ones is when a patient suffers from a cancer phobia. This may have been triggered by something like a close friend or family member being diagnosed with cancer, and sometimes, it is one manifestation of a more generalised anxiety state, but sometimes, there is no obvious cause, and, on occasions, it may be delusional.

When I was working in the casualty department at Newcastle General Hospital, a man came in, saying that he had a tumour in his mouth. He attempted to show me, but there was nothing abnormal to see, and I did my best to reassure him and sent him on his way. A few days later, he returned at a different time of day, but as I was working shifts, I happened to be on duty again, so I spent a further few minutes peering into every corner of his mouth looking for the mysterious tumour, which, of course, wasn't there.

He seemed unconvinced by my reassurance but did leave, only to return a third time—at night, on this occasion, only to be greeted by yours truly once more! After this, I think he either gave up or went to a different hospital because he did not come back to us. I think he concluded I was the only doctor who worked there and that I wasn't taking his concerns seriously. Of course, one has to be very careful; as a patient once said to me, "Just because you are a hypochondriac, it doesn't mean there isn't something wrong with you."

A number of years ago, my daughter bought me a mug for my birthday, which is shown in the photograph below, and I try to place it prominently on my desk, but as most of my patients do not speak English (and most do not use Google), it is primarily for the benefit of the expats!

I really must mention the final patient that I have learnt a lot from, namely myself! Many people consider that it is a useful experience for a doctor to be a

"Google search" mug

patient, and this certainly widens one's perspective. I have been a patient on a few occasions, thankfully not for anything serious.

The most significant was when I was working in Bishop Auckland. I suddenly developed a severe left-sided abdominal pain one evening, which I self-diagnosed as ureteric colic due to a kidney stone. I was at home but was the consultant on-call, so technically, I had to admit myself to the hospital! Fortunately, one of my colleagues came to the rescue and treated me.

The journey to the hospital was interesting as we had to stop en-route so I could leap out of the car to vomit. I was admitted overnight and managed to avoid being seen by most of my current patients on the ward as there was a spare side-room. At least my diagnosis proved to be correct, and I had possibly developed it as a result of my love of long-distance running with a tendency to become dehydrated through not drinking enough water.

My main memories of the event were the effects of having a pethidine injection (similar to morphine) which did not seem to stop the pain but produced a curious detachment from it so that it no longer appeared to be a problem and then being wheeled down the corridors on a trolley, watching the ceiling go by, on the way to have an X-ray. This created a feeling of not really being in control of things as I had only ever walked down the same corridors.

One of my other experiences was for a minor surgical procedure on my throat on the Isle of Man, and here, my most notable memory was the weird, but not unpleasant, experience of having a general anaesthetic. The strangest thing was going to sleep in one place and waking up—apparently immediately thereafter, in another bed. I was also somewhat incoherent, according to my son, who was sitting by the bed and informed me that I kept saying the same things over and over. At least I wasn't one of the people that comes round and becomes disorientated or violent and starts trying to jump out of bed.

Chapter 10
Naughty Stuff

I was in two minds whether to include this chapter at all as it details various pranks that we used to play during our many hours spent in and around the hospitals as junior doctors. Let me begin with a disclaimer, hopefully not repeating myself too much, but things were very different 40 years ago from how they are now.

Most of the things we got up to would be unthinkable now, and I inwardly cringe as I remember some of them. In fact, they would no doubt lead to disciplinary action, but I am hoping that some sort of Statute of Limitations applies here—especially as I now work abroad and only in a voluntary capacity (although the General Medical Council does list me as being in good standing, and you are safe as I have voluntarily relinquished my licence to practise in the UK). I will try to ensure that no details that would allow anyone else to be identified are included but if, by any chance you are reading this—you know who you are!

A common trick played on new student nurses who were working on the wards for the first time was to send them down to the hospital stores and ask for a long stand which they invariably received or similar non-existent items, and this was just a harmless bit of fun. Of course, this is not exclusive to the medical and nursing professions, so left-handed screwdrivers, sky hooks and so on are oft sought after items. Medical students would often be caught out in similar ways, although sometimes, the trap was more elaborate.

I remember one surgeon who would demonstrate a way of detecting fluid in the abdominal cavity called shifting dullness. This consisted of tapping on one of your fingers placed on the patient's abdomen (percussing to use the medical term) in different places and listening to the sound produced and, in particular, whether it was resonant (hollow sound) or dull (more like a thud). Once the demarcation between the two had been identified, the patient was asked to turn onto one side, and the procedure repeated.

If there was fluid present (creating the dull sound), it would move with gravity, and the loops of intestine (creating the resonant sound) would float up to the top, thus moving the line of demarcation (hence shifting dullness). It was not uncommon for the most junior students to be unaware of this, so when he asked what the sign was called, he would get a series of blank expressions. At this point, the trap was laid, and he then said, "OK. so and so, just go over to the other side of the ward." Once they were there, he would say, "OK, now come back here," then he would say, "See—shifting dullness!" Ritual humiliation of medical students was just seen as part of the educational process and a goad to stimulate conscientious study, but now, of course, it would be labelled bullying!

I have previously mentioned the importance of the doctor's mess in those days when we all worked in 'firms', where each consultant would have his own junior staff and set of patients—trainees of varying levels of seniority with the more junior doctors often living in hospital accommodation on site. One of the popular events were mess parties which were arranged at various intervals, mostly at weekends. I was only involved in the organisation of one of these, at Shotley Bridge Hospital in County Durham. We decided it would be entertaining to hold a cocktail party. I had recently discovered that they were enjoyable to consume and fun to make. I had a book of recipes and a cocktail shaker so what more did we need?

Well, we certainly needed ingredients, and as we had sold tickets in advance, we knew the sort of numbers of people to expect. Several of us went to the local off-licence to buy huge quantities of all the usual spirits and some of the less common ingredients such as Angostura Bitters, Blue Curacao and Galliano. I had also concocted my own recipe, stealing the name from Douglas Adams' wonderful book, 'A Hitchhiker's Guide to the Galaxy'. Fans of the book will already know that this was the pan-galactic gargle blaster. This was described in the book as the best drink in the universe and the effect was like having your brains smashed out with a slice of lemon wrapped round a large gold brick!

If you have not read his book, you should stop reading this one immediately and go and read it—I think it is one of the funniest and cleverest books I have ever read. Although in the BBC production, the drink was actually a pale green colour, and my own version looked exactly like methylated spirits—purple; however, I think the effects were probably similar. Because the tickets were all prepaid, it was an open bar and I and some friends spent the next few hours happily mixing the drinks and dishing them out. No one had actually drunk cocktails before and, as I am sure most people know nowadays, the more exotic ones were quite sweet and did not taste particularly strong, but this was deceptive and after the first hour or so, the alcohol kicked in, and suddenly, there were a lot of very tipsy people in the room.

By two hours, most were frankly drunk and became increasingly rowdy! I was able to observe the process as I abstained from the drinks so that I could be co-ordinated enough to mix them. There was no bad behaviour, and nothing was broken, just a lot of hangovers the following day. But overall, it was judged to have been a great success. I'm not sure what the average alcohol consumption per person was, but we had an awful lot of empty bottles of spirits to clear up at the end.

Sometimes, the parties were held off premises, and I remember going to one fancy dress party in Newcastle wearing a 'Spotty Dog' outfit—this was a character from one of my childhood TV favourites called The Woodentops, and it was basically a dalmatian dog puppet, so I was covered with black spots on my white clothes and face. When I arrived at the venue (a pub), I went into the bar where there seemed to be a party going on. I asked someone if they knew where the fancy dress party was. They said they didn't, but to let them know when I found it as it looked as if it was going to be more fun than the one they were at.

Spending so much time on the wards as a junior doctor, one inevitably got to know the other staff even though most of the jobs were only for six months or a year. The other staff were usually working at the hospital on a long-term basis so had to become acquainted with new doctors on a frequent basis. I think some of the staff got a bit fed up with the constant changeover and having to get to know the new set of doctors' peculiarities, whereas others seemed to relish the prospect.

One nurse in particular became good friends with me, and we were always having a laugh together when the ward was quiet. We had also joked about spiking each other's drinks with various medicines. One weekend, I was off duty and was going to go shopping in the town a mile or so away, but I met her for a coffee in the canteen first. I had decided that today was the day to add the diuretic to her coffee (a diuretic is a medicine that makes you pass a lot of urine). Unfortunately, unbeknownst to me, she had decided exactly the same thing, and so, we both drank our frusemide-laden coffees with a hidden smirk. I then went into town, and she returned to the ward.

30 minutes later, I was already starting to feel uncomfortable from my rapidly filling bladder, and at this point, discovered that there did not appear to be any public toilets in the vicinity. As I became increasingly desperate, I had to abandon the shopping trip and rush back to the hospital before I had an unfortunate accident. Had I been in Cambodia, I could have merely chosen any convenient wall or patch of grass to pee. She, on the other hand, had to keep making excuses to leave the ward to go to the toilet for the rest of the morning. For a while, I wondered whether our coffees had somehow got mixed up. It was when we next met that it became clear that we had both done exactly the same thing to each other!

A more complicated prank involved a female house officer who was an excellent doctor, but a little flighty. I'm not sure why we (that is, the nursing staff of the surgical ward and myself) decided to select her as the unfortunate recipient of our devious plan, but she turned out to be the perfect person. If a patient died on the ward, one of the first things to happen (assuming there was no CPR) was for the doctor to come and certify the death. One of the tests we used was to look into the back of the eye using an instrument called an ophthalmoscope to look for so-called venous trucking—this was when you could see segments of blood stationary within the retinal veins and indicated that there was no blood flow. This involved getting very close to the deceased in order to see clearly.

I was working as the registrar on this particular ward, and we used to have a handover to the staff who were going to be on duty overnight to highlight any patients who were particularly sick and so on. During the handover, I explained that there was a terminally ill patient in a side-room on the ward, whom we fully expected to die overnight, and for whom, no attempts to resuscitate should be made.

"You will just need to certify the death if the ward calls you," I explained.

Later that evening, I went to the empty side-room and put on surgical scrubs (similar to the pyjamas worn by patients), and the nursing staff then proceeded to coat my hair and face with talc and water to make me look old and very pale. We completed the illusion with a nasogastric tube taped to my nose and an intravenous infusion apparently connected to my arm. They then covered me with a shroud and put the light onto the night setting, which meant everything was gloomy (this was necessary for the eye examination, anyway).

Then, they called the house officer and said so and so had died, so please would you come and certify the body. A few minutes later, she pitched up—the nurses told her they had already checked that my pulse was absent, so she picked up the ophthalmoscope and pulled back the shroud covering my head.

Needless to say, she did not recognise me, and just before she opened my eye to peer in, I opened both my eyes wide and said boo. I think she actually left the floor as she jumped back in horror before realisation set in as to what had happened. I am pleased to say that she took it extremely well and did see the funny side (once she had had a chance to calm down).

I know it was cruel, but I will never forget the look on her face. She did get her own back on me a little as she grabbed the big jug of drinking water on the bedside cabinet and threw it over me. It is perhaps amazing that we all grew up to be such normal, well-balanced people!

Reflecting on all these experiences has made me realise what an epic journey it has been for me, and it is with a true sense of gratitude that I look back over my career. I trust there is more to come—I am still seeing patients on a regular basis, so I have little doubt there will be more surprises in store, but my focus is now on training the next generation of surgeons in Cambodia, and my prayer is that they will follow the advice I myself was given and adopt my good habits but avoid my bad ones.

Printed in Great Britain
by Amazon